CRITERION THEATRE
presents
TWO ONE-ACT PLAYS

TAKING PART

by ADAM BRACE

AFTER THE PARTY

by SERGE CARTWRIGHT

27 July to 12 August 2012

Presented as part of *Playing the Games*.

Playing the Games is a two-week programme of new theatre, comedy, lunchtime talks and late-night storytelling.

Notes from the Producer

It is a rare thing these days for playwrights to be writing new work directly for a West End theatre. It's even rarer that those playwrights are young and not widely known. These are the reasons that it gives me such pleasure to commission, develop and produce new one-act plays by Adam Brace and Serge Cartwright. We approached a number of playwrights to pitch responses to this unique moment in history – when the Olympic Games come to London. Two stood out and whilst complementary, look at the Games from two very different perspectives. Serge's *After the Party* is a play about London and Londoners – two men who have grown up in Stratford, a now fast-changing landscape. Adam's *Taking Part* looks at the arrival of a Congolese swimmer in London with his Russian coach, both of them arriving with their own socio-cultural preconceptions. What binds both plays, other than the backdrop of the Olympic Games, is an interrogation of what it means to be British.

I'm also thrilled to have had the chance to invite the brilliant Charlotte Gwinner on board to direct Adam's play as well as a stellar design team, comprising James Cotterill, Greg Clarke, Emma Chapman and Joshua Carr.

The context for the two plays is 'Playing the Games', a two-week programme of lunchtime talks, late night comedy, storytelling and new theatre. I've had the privilege of co-curating this season with Stephen Fry, the Criterion Theatre Trust's chairman, to whom I am very thankful, and I look forward to welcoming an extraordinary mix of comedians, Olympian greats of past and present, and world-renowned actors to the Criterion stage.

Finally, a huge amount of gratitude to my right-hand woman Natalie Macaluso, Fiona Callaghan and the rest of the Criterion staff who have worked over and beyond to deliver this ambitious programme. And, of course, to Sally Greene and the board of the Criterion Theatre Trust for their support and belief.

Samuel Hodges

Taking Part was first performed at The Criterion Theatre
on 29 July 2012.

    Cast
    HENRY   Obi Abili
    GRIGORY   Paul Moriarty

The action takes place in Kinshasa, Democratic Republic of Congo,
and London, 2012.

After the Party was first performed at The Criterion Theatre
on 29 July 2012.

    Cast
    CHELLE   Sophie Cosson
    RAY   David Fynn
    KEITH/MIDWIFE   Malcolm Hamilton
    CARMELA/NATALIE Kate Lamb
    SEAN   Richard Ridell

The action takes place in Stratford, London, 2012.

    Creative team
    Director of *Taking Part*   Charlotte Gwinner
    Director of *After the Party* Samuel Hodges
    Designer   James Cotterill
    Lighting Designer   Emma Chapman
    Assistant Lighting Designer Joshua Carr
    Sound Designer   Gregory Clarke
    Casting Director   Camilla Evans

TAKING PART
BY ADAM BRACE

OBI ABILI | HENRY
Theatre Credits include: *Play House* (The Orange Tree); *Sixty-Six Books* (Bush Theatre); *Six Degrees Of Separation* (Old Vic*); Dido Queen of Carthage* (National Theatre); *The Brothers Size* (Young Vic Theatre/ATC); *Angels In America* (Lyric Hammersmith/Headlong Theatre); *Fabulation and Darfur: How Long is Never* (Tricycle Theatre).
Film Credits Include: Marc Forster's *World War Z*, Michael Hoffman's *Gambit*.
Television Credits Include: *Strikeback II*, *Injustice*, *Nativity*, *Foyles War*, *The Take*, *Moses Jones*, *Kingdom*, *Ten Days to War*, *Life is Wild*, *Afterlife*.
Obi graduated from The Royal Academy of Dramatic Art in July 2006.

PAUL MORIARTY | GRIGORY
Theatre Credits include: *Titanic* (Belfast MAC); *Translations* (Curve Theatre); *Nineteen Eighty Four* (Manchester Royal Exchange); *Sus* (Young Vic); *Rosmersholm, Richard II, Coriolanus,* (Almeida Theatre); *The Elephant Man* (National Tour); *Saved* (Abbey Theatre Dublin); *A View from the Bridge* (Sheffield Crucible); *Serious Money* (Wyndhams and New York); *Love and Money* (Manchester Royal Exchange); *Market Boy, Pillars of the Community, Sing Yer Heart Out For The Lads, Macbeth, Black Snow, As I Lay Dying, The Crucible, Racing Demon, Absence of War,* (National Theatre); *Kingfisher Blue* (Bush Theatre); *King Lear, Penny For A Song, Antony and Cleopatra, Troilus and Cressida, Bingo* (Royal Shakespeare Company).
Film Credits Include: *Hidden Agenda*.
Television Credits Include: *Ashes to Ashes, Holby City, Jack of Hearts, EastEnders, A Touch of Frost, The Knock, Murder Most Horrid, Pride and Prejudice, Wycliffe, Shine on Harvey Moon*.

ADAM BRACE | PLAYWRIGHT

Adam Brace was born in London in 1980. He studied Drama at Kent and Writing for Performance (MA) at Goldsmiths. His first full-length play *Stovepipe* transferred from the HighTide Festival to London in collaboration with the National Theatre and the Bush. Shorter plays include *A Real Humane Person Who Cares and All That* (Hill St, Edinburgh/Arcola, London) and *Midnight Your Time* with Diana Quick (HighTide Festival/Assembly, Edinburgh). In 2011 he co-wrote and co-directed *The Four Stages of Cruelty* with Seb Armesto, based on Hogarth's engravings, at the Arcola. Adam is under commission to Headlong and the National Theatre, and is an Associate at the Gate Theatre, Notting Hill. He also writes for and directs live comedy.

CHARLOTTE GWINNER | DIRECTOR

Charlotte was Associate Director at The Bush from 2009-2011 where she directed *Our New Girl*, *Little Dolls,* both by Nancy Harris, *50 Ways to Leave Your Lover* and *The Knowledge* by John Donnelly. Further directing credits include: *Benefactors* as part of the Michael Frayn season at Sheffield Crucible, *Knives and Hens* at the Ustinov Bath Theatre Royal, *The Confederate* for the Trafalgar Studios, *Men Should Weep* for Oxford Stage Company/The Citizens Theatre, *The Blood of Others* for the Arcola, *The Country of The Blind* for the Gate Theatre. She is Artistic Director and Founder of award-winning company ANGLE Theatre, most recently producing its second season 'ANGLE at the Bush' at the Bush.

AFTER THE PARTY
BY SERGE CARTWRIGHT

SOPHIE COSSON I CHELLE

Theatre includes: *The Changeling* (Southwark Playhouse); *Much Ado About Nothing* (International Tour); *Two Women* (Theatre Royal Stratford East); *The Comedy Of Errors* (Sell A Door); *Only Human* (Theatre503).

Television Includes: *Doctor Who*, *Call the Midwife*.

Radio Includes: *The Wire*, *The Archers* (BBC).

Sophie trained at the Guildford School of Acting on a full three-year scholarship. She was a recipient of the Sir John Gielgud and Sir Michael Redgrave Bursaries.

DAVID FYNN I RAY

Theatre includes: *She Stoops to Conquer*, *Romeo and Juliet* (National Theatre); *25th Annual Putnam County Spelling Bee* (Donmar Warehouse); *Dry Write Presents…What's in the Box?* (The Bush); *Mojo* (RSC); *Thunderer* (Edinburgh); *All My Sons* (Leicester Curve); *Trainspotting* (New Leicester Square Theatre); *Toys* (New Leicester Square Theatre); *Starved* (Theatre503); *Tickledom*.

Film Includes: *King of Soho, Deviation, Sonambulists, Leap Year, Trackdown*.

Television Includes: *Big Bad World, Game of Thrones, Mayday, Parents, The Black Mirror, Life's Too Short, Pete Vs Life, Doctor Who, Doctors, PEEP SHOW, The Inbetweeners, Spooks*.

MALCOLM HAMILTON I KEITH/MIDWIFE

Theatre Credits include: *The Crowstarver* (Theatre Alibi); *The Morpeth Carol* (Sleepdogs/ Bristol Ferment); *Digits* (Tobacco Factory); *My Green Your Grey* (Bristol Old Vic); *Dead Pan* (The Arches); *Emily's House* (Visible Fictions); *Twelfth Night, Peter Pan* (Perth Theatre) and his self-penned solo show *The Station: Fourstones* (The Idle Dream).

Film Includes: *Detour, Eilmer*.

Radio Includes: *Chess Girls, Paradise Place, Beyond Black, Beasts on the Lawn* (BBC).

Malcolm trained at Queen Margaret College, Edinburgh.

KATE LAMB | CARMELA/ NATALIE

Theatre Credits include: *Summer and Smoke* (Southwark Playhouse); *How to be Happy, The Conspirators* (Orange Tree Theatre).

Film Includes: *Caught in Flight.*

Television includes: *Mayday, Silk, Doctors, Switch.*

Kate recently graduated from London Academy of Music and Dramatic Arts.

RICHARD RIDDELL | SEAN

Theatre includes: *The Homecoming, The Merchant of Venice* (RSC). *Filumena* (Almeida); *The Comedy Of Errors, Titus Andronicus* (Shakespeare's Globe).

Film includes: *Weekender, Blitz, Robin Hood, The Imaginarium Of Doctor Parnassus, Act Of God, Northern star: a love story, Enemy Lines.*

Television includes: *A Warriors Tale, Misfits, The Fattest Man In Britain, Merlin, Krod Mandoon, Fanny Hill, Waking The Dead, Heart Beat.*

Richard graduated from The Royal Academy of Dramatic Art in 2006.

SERGE CARTWRIGHT | PLAYWRIGHT

After university, Serge became a television journalist in London and then worked for a year at 'Russia Today' in Moscow, an English-language TV station backed by the Kremlin. This experience formed the basis of his play *Moscow Live*, which was produced by HighTide in 2010 and went on to be shortlisted for the prestigious John Whiting Award. Serge then moved back to London where he wrote *The Matter in Hand*, which was longlisted for the Bruntwood Prize, Britain's biggest award for playwriting.

SAMUEL HODGES | DIRECTOR

Samuel Hodges is the Producer at the Criterion Theatre. Before joining the Criterion last year, he was the Artistic Director of HighTide Festival Theatre, which he founded in 2006. For HighTide he programmed five festivals, produced over 25 plays internationally and launched the Old Vic Tunnels. For the Criterion, in October last year Hodges launched *Criterion Presents*, a series of shows, events and panel discussions that run alongside *The 39 Steps*. He also conceived and directed the *Stories Before Bedtime* series which featured Mark Gatiss, Tom Hiddleston, Russell Tovey, Andrew Scott and Billy Boyd. Sam wrote the award-winning short film *Player*, starring Pete Postlethwaite and Celia Imrie, and wrote and directed *Double Take*, a short dance film commissioned as part of the Big Dance programme for Channel 4.

JAMES COTTERILL | DESIGNER

Recent designs include; *Good*, *A View from the Bridge*, *Powder Monkey*, *Mojo Mickybo* (Royal Exchange Theatre); *Straight*, *The Pride*, *That Face* (Crucible Studio); *The Seven Year Itch* (Salisbury Playhouse); *Macbeth*, *The Demolition Man (Bolton Octagon); Accolade* (FinboroughTheatre); *The Flint Street Nativity*, *The Elves And The Shoemaker* (Hull Truck); *The Wages of Thin* (Old Red Lion – OffWest End.Com Nomination for Best Set); *Estate Walls* (Oval House). In 2005 he was a winner of The Linbury Prize for Stage Design for *Not The End Of The World* at Bristol Old Vic. In 2009 his installation *Smash Here* was chosen by *Time Out* to be part of the Deloitte Ignite festival at the Royal Opera House.

EMMA CHAPMAN | LIGHTING DESIGNER

Theatre includes: *Run!* (Polka Theatre); *Sex with a Stranger* (Trafalgar Studios); *Dublin Carol* (Donmar season Trafalgar Studios); *The Sea Plays* (Old Vic Tunnels); *Parallel Hamlet* (Young Vic); *Dick Whittington* (Bury St Edmund); *Roundabout* (Sheffield); *Rose* (Edinburgh); *The Mountaintop* (Theatre503 and Trafalgar Studios); *The Painter* (Arcola Theatre); *Wet Weather Cover* (King's Head and Arts Theatres); *The Machine Gunners* (Polka Theatre). Opera includes: *Xerxes, Carmen* (Royal Northern College of Music, Manchester); *Così fan tutte* (Royal College of Music); *The Pied Piper* (Opera North); *Rumplestiltskin* (London Children's Ballet, Peacock Theatre), available on DVD.

JOSHUA CARR | ASSISTANT LIGHTING DESIGNER

Joshua Carr Trained at RADA in Lighting Design and stage electrics. As Lighting Designer: HighTide Festival; *Stage Fright* (Theatre Royal Bury St Edmunds); *Port Authority* (Southwark Playhouse); *Dick Whittington* (Stafford Gatehouse); *His Teeth* (Only Connect); *Love of a Nightingale* (Fourth Monkey); *Threepenny Opera* (Fourth Monkey); *Antigone* (Fourth Monkey); *The Song of Deborah* (The Lowry Studio 1); *The Shape of things* (The Soho Gallery). As Production Electrician: *The Sea Plays* (The Old Vic Tunnels); *HighTide Festival 2011* (The Cut); *The Painter* (The New Arcola 1); *The Maddening Rain* (Old Red Lion Theatre); *The Hostage* (Southwark Play-house). As Assistant Lighting Designer: *Xerxes* (Royal Northern College of Music); *Rose* (Pleasant); *Lake Boat & Prarie du Chien* (Arcola 2); *Lidless* (Trafalgar 2); *Ditch* (The Old Vic Tunnels).

GREGORY CLARKE | SOUND DESIGNER

Theatre Credits include: *Misterman, Twelfth Night, No Man's Land, Tristan and Yseult, The Emperor Jones* and *Earthquakes in London* (National Theatre); *The Heart Of Robin Hood, Great Expectations, Coriolanus, The Merry Wives of Windsor, Tantalus, Cymbeline, The Merchant of Venice* and *A Midsummer Nights' Dream* (Royal Shakespeare Company); *Pygmalion* and *The Philanthropist* (American Airlines, Broadway); *A Flea In Her Ear, National Anthems* and *Six Degrees of Separation* (Old Vic). West End credits include: *A Voyage Round My Father, The Vortex, Cloud Nine, The Philanthropist, Some Girls, Waiting For Godot, What the Butler Saw, The Dresser, Amy's View, You Never Can Tell, Betrayal, Abigail's Party, Journeys End, Equus* and *Bedroom Farce.*

Gregory won a Tony Award for Best Sound Design in a Play for *Equus* and the New York Drama Desk Award for Outstanding Sound Design for *Journey's End.*

SIMON MONEY I DIALECT COACH

Simon is a professional voice & accent coach who spent two years apprenticed to renowned voice coach Patsy Rodenburg at the Guildhall School of Music & Drama. He works in theatre, TV, film & with private clients. Recent projects include the world premiere of *SUM* at the Royal Opera House Covent Garden; *Mack & Mabel* at the Southwark Playhouse; *Dancing at Lughnasa* at the Mercury Theatre, Colchester; and is about to start work on *Lost in Yonkers* at the Watford Palace Theatre. He teaches at GSMD, Actorworks, YPTC and the London Dramatic Academy.

NATALIE MACALUSO I ASSISTANT PRODUCER

Trained at The Oxford School of Drama. She is currently Assistant Producer at the Criterion Theatre. As Producer, theatre includes: *Abigail's Party* (Wyndham's Theatre); *His Greatness* (Finborough Theatre); *Pippin* (Menier Chocolate Factory); *The Taming of the Shrew*, *The Rover* (Southwark Playhouse); The 24 Hour Plays (Old Vic New Voices at The Old Vic). Radio Production includes: *The Afghan and the Penguin*, *Waves Breaking on a Shore* (Promenade Productions for BBC Radio 4). Natalie is an alumni of the Old Vic TS Eliot US/UK Exchange 2011.

Production Credits

Production Manager	Tim Highman
Deputy Stage Manager	Julie Whitcombe – *Taking Part*
Deputy Stage Manager	Demelza Fry – *After The Party*
Assistant Stage Manager	Nikki Gooch
Costume Supervisor	Sharna David
Dialect Coach	Simon Money
Musical Consultant	Laurence Allen
Board Operator	Chris Packham
Showman	Alex Hawkins
Marketing	Kym Bartlett LTD
Press	Premier PR
Poster & Graphic Design	Samuel Muir
Production Photographer	Bill Knight

Criterion Theatre

General Manager	Fiona Callaghan
Producer	Samuel Hodges
Assistant Producer	Natalie Macaluso
Theatre Manager	Alex Browne
Assistant Theatre Manager	Daniela Lama
Box Office Manager	Alec Connell
Deputy Box Office Manager	Alun Hood
Box Office Assistants	David Gore
	Gemma Bealing
Master Carpenter	Simon Renton
Deputy Master Carpenter	John Schwartz-Holford
Chief Electrician	Tim Ingram
Deputy Chief Electrician	Chris Barham
Charge Hand	Adam King
Education Co-ordinator	Catrin Lowe
Chairman	Stephen Fry
Chief Executive	Sally Greene
Directors	Peter Clayton
	Joyce Hytner
	Alan Baines
	Robert Bourne
Finance Director	Conor Marren

PLAYING THE GAMES
EDUCATION PROGRAMME
From East End to West End

Picking up on the growing buzz in the city, this summer we are bringing young people together in our West End venue to celebrate the world's foremost sports competition in our new community and learning programme *From East End to West End*.

We are giving young people an outlet to express the feelings that a major event like this provokes through the art of theatre making, as well as giving them an opportunity to watch a brand new play and hear from (and maybe even meet) their sporting heroes.

Free tickets will be on offer to see *After the Party* and *Taking Part*, as well as participation in a bespoke workshop.

We are also offering young people the opportunity to be part of the audience at our lunchtime interviews, where past and present Olympians are taking to the stage for a series of discussions about their life and work. Hosted by television and stage personalities the line-up includes Stephen Fry, Rick Edwards, Stephen Daldry and Clive Owen interviewing Edwin Moses, Haile Gebrselassie, Kriss Akabusi and Adrien Nyonshuti.

The Criterion Theatre would like to say a very special thank you to the following people, whose help and support has been invaluable:

David Mitchell & Caroline Heale from GSA – Guildford School of Acting – for the loan of their lighting desk. www.conservatoire.org.

Sheila Beckerleg.

Waterloo Brasserie.

Nick Giles and Shoreditch Town Hall.

The Scenery Shop.

Sound equipment supplied, with generous support, by Stage Sound Services.

Edward Snape, Marilyn Eardley, Fran Rafferty and all at Fiery Angel.

Jasper Fox, the stage management team and company of *The 39 Steps*.

ALFRED
HITCHCOCK'S

'THE

39

STEPS'

'THEATRICAL
GOLD'
STEPHEN FRY

CRITERION
THEATRE

0844 847 1778 love39steps.com
CRITERION THEATRE PICCADILLY CIRCUS W1

PLAYING THE GAMES

TAKING PART
by ADAM BRACE

AFTER THE PARTY
by SERGE CARTWRIGHT

OBERON BOOKS
LONDON

WWW.OBERONBOOKS.COM

First published in 2012 by Oberon Books Ltd
521 Caledonian Road, London N7 9RH
Tel: +44 (0) 20 7607 3637 / Fax: +44 (0) 20 7607 3629
e-mail: info@oberonbooks.com
www.oberonbooks.com

Visit www.oberonbooks.com to read more about all our books
and to buy them. You will also find features, author interviews and
news of any author events, and you can sign up for e-newsletters
so that you're always first to hear about our new releases.

Contents

TAKING PART

This play is dedicated to Vicky Jones.

Many thanks to:

Rosie Cobbe for her patience and support, Sebastian Born who
helped me go to DRC, Sergei Gratchev who helped me live
in Moscow, Annie Matunda with whom I stayed in Kinshasa,
Marie-Claire Faray, Sam Hodges, Nikki and Nigel Hopkins, Sasha
Antonov, Dan Usztan, Diane Brace, Andrew Walby at Oberon,
Chris Kelham and Tom Oldroyd and my long-suffering landlords
the Joneses.

□ *Empty silence, nothing to be said*

■ *Full silence, something actively not said*

1.

HENRY, a Congolese man in a swimming suit and goggles.

He has a pen, practising an interview.

HENRY   My name is Lucky Henry.
No no. No translation please.
I am fluent in Swahili, Lingala, French and English.
Yes?
Why do people call me this?
People call me Lucky Henry because.
Because I have survived many horrors.
And every time in my life I make the best. Of the situation.
Sorry, at the back?
My Olympic dream was started when uh Grigory Ser

He checks a name.

Grigory Sergeyevich Polonsky arrive in Congo to be my coach.

2.

HENRY is on a starting block, preparing for a race.

The Beeper sounds and he falls forward into darkness.

GRIGORY, a Russian man in a bandana, watches.

3.

HENRY, dripping wet. A towel.
GRIGORY enters, smoking.

GRIGORY Henry?

      □

HENRY   No!

GRIGORY I am Grigory.

HENRY   No! You are here!

GRIGORY Please to meet you.

HENRY   A great great honour.
I thought we are meeting at your hotel.

GRIGORY This my hotel.

HENRY You are staying at Intercontinental.

GRIGORY I change hotel.

HENRY Why?

GRIGORY They say you are train in this hotel pool.

HENRY Yes but the Intercontinental is better hotel.

GRIGORY Really?

HENRY For sure.

GRIGORY It's the same.

HENRY No it's better.

GRIGORY Same only more men with guns.

HENRY Exactly, better.

GRIGORY How was your swim Henry?

HENRY Everyone calls me Lucky Henry.

GRIGORY Okay.
Your swim.

HENRY It is a great honour to have you in Congo Monsieur Grigory, my heart is full of hopes, I will do everything I can to win a medal for Congo.

GRIGORY Henry

HENRY Together we do great work.

GRIGORY How was the swim today?

HENRY Good Grigory, feeling good, I love being in the water, the water is for me like a second skin, my wife will tell you I love being in the water almost as much as being in her arms. Actually sometimes more but I can't say this to her! I love this hat.

GRIGORY Bandana.

HENRY Yes.

GRIGORY Sweat.

HENRY Again?

GRIGORY It's for sweat.

HENRY   Ah yes, hot country.

GRIGORY Your swim.

HENRY   You work in hot country before?

GRIGORY Every job, always fucking hot country.

HENRY   Where?

GRIGORY Thailand, Korea, Mozambique. I love cold country.

HENRY   London is cold.

GRIGORY I know, my son live in London – was your / swim good

HENRY   Maybe we can visit him at the Olympics?

GRIGORY Henry the swim was good for you today?

HENRY   Yeah feeling good – how long you watch for?

GRIGORY Thirty minutes.

HENRY   Ah, Lord, you watch a long time.

GRIGORY You're happy with training?

HENRY   I'm always happy, I am Lucky Henry. En Francais c'est Hereux Henri, it can be translated as Happy Henry or Lucky Henry, I prefer Lucky but both are true

GRIGORY By your standard, freestyle was acceptable?

HENRY   For me today is about Grigory, welcoming you, my new coach – it's a dream that you come here. I am living a dream, thank you.

GRIGORY Don't thank me, please, it's IOC money.

HENRY   Ha ha, I Thank God for the Olympic Committee. With your help, I can win a medal for Congo.

GRIGORY Henry today's swim, it was slow?

HENRY   I always try, but with you I will be much faster.

GRIGORY I cannot grow for you a tail.

                    □

HENRY   Sorry I didn't understand.

GRIGORY You are very slow.

HENRY   Okay Coach.

☐

GRIGORY Very slow Henry.

HENRY   Okay Coach.

GRIGORY Your time. When I agree to work with you. Your time is fifteen seconds shorter.

HENRY   There was no timing today.

GRIGORY I have watch.

HENRY   Maybe I was slow today.

GRIGORY Not maybe.

HENRY   Tomorrow I'll be better.

GRIGORY Not better fifteen seconds.
The printed time I have for you – fifteen seconds shorter.

HENRY   I think the printed time they give you is not my time.

GRIGORY No because your time, your true time, is very fucking slow.

■

Sorry.
But you cannot be help.

HENRY   You don't understand, but I will explain. I have never had a chance for a proper coach. I am Lucky Henry because in my life I have always come through the difficult problems. I have escape from hell. God looks down on me and I want to honour him. I race for him, like – you watch English cinema?

GRIGORY Yah, sure.

HENRY   Not cinema in English but actually from England.

GRIGORY Oh.
No.

HENRY   The movie Chariots of Fire. I race for God and my country, to help

GRIGORY I dunno this fucking movie Henry, but you are too slow to be coach.
I'm sorry for this. But I must say to you now.
Tomorrow I fly home.

HENRY   I am Lucky Henry.

GRIGORY An incorrect time was submit. I came here believing you were only little slow, but Henry?

HENRY   Yes Coach.

GRIGORY You are very slow.

HENRY   Okay thank you Coach. I will prove you wrong.

GRIGORY I leave tomorrow.

HENRY   One chance.

GRIGORY I have maybe one job before I retire Lucky Henry, I am sorry, it is not you.
I am angry. Not with you.
But I am angry.
I come long way to shit fuck Africa. For nothing.
I wish you health and happiness in the world. But this is fucked.

GRIGORY leaves.

4.

GRIGORY's hotel room.

GRIGORY is speaking into his room phone.

GRIGORY Yah.
Very soon please.
Thank you.

GRIGORY calls to outside the room.

They are coming.
Henry?
Security are coming.

☐

Henry are you gone?

☐

☐

HENRY   No I'm still here.

GRIGORY I call the guard.

HENRY   I know.

GRIGORY They are coming.

HENRY   The security are my friends.
             They know I am here. I am Lucky Henry.

                    ☐

                    ☐

GRIGORY This is not normal in my country Henry.

HENRY   Okay.
             Well.
             It's not normal here also.

                    ☐

             I am not mad Coach. One conversation.

GRIGORY Whatever you say, I fly home.

                    ☐

                    ☐

                    ☐

                    ■

             Do you have gun?

HENRY   For sure.

GRIGORY Henry please you must leave!

HENRY   Oh I mean, at my house.

                    ☐

    GRIGORY goes to let him in, but stops.

GRIGORY This is very difficult for me, this is new country, with many
            problems. So, I am worry, you understand.

HENRY   I understand Coach.

    GRIGORY lets him in warily.

GRIGORY Please. You have no chance.
            You are not swimmer Henry.
            Please go home.

HENRY   I would like to be friends.
              I am not dangereux

GRIGORY Somebody lie to me. About your time.

HENRY   The mistake of the time is not my fault. This is Congo.

GRIGORY Sure.

HENRY   Congo is mistakes.

GRIGORY Sure.

HENRY   It is a misprint by the DRC Olympic Committee.

GRIGORY Whatever, you have no chance.

HENRY   For why?

GRIGORY Because. Everything is wrong.

HENRY   What things are wrong?

GRIGORY Your hands, your feet, your breathing, agility. Your stroke rate.
            Your start your turn. And really all of your swimming.

              ☐

HENRY   Is this how you normally coach?
              Because it is not very nice.

              ☐

GRIGORY Your arms are levers like in machine, arms out please.
            Distance from the rotation axis, here is the key – short lever
            gives smaller resistance arm, and therefore mechanically
            advantageous, but bad for high velocity movement. Your
            levers good for longer swimming, you should swim a longer
            event. But your aerobic fitness is not good for this. What size
            your feet?

HENRY   Twelve.

GRIGORY European or American?

HENRY   The shoes? Chinese.

GRIGORY You have Chinese shoes?

HENRY   Yes. Everything here is Chinese.

*GRIGORY takes one of HENRY's feet so HENRY is hopping. GRIGORY inspects
and places his hand against it.*

GRIGORY Yah. Never never never.

HENRY   These are big feet.

GRIGORY But not right proportion.

HENRY   Please can I have my foot?

GRIGORY Hands?
             Actually your hands okay.

HENRY   I have a heart and I have Jesus love.

GRIGORY And you're twenty-seven? Three years after your peak.
             You are catastrophe for swimming Henry.
             You are very charming catastrophe and I wish I can help you.
             But is not possible.

                    □

HENRY   So okay. It is a challenge.
             But.
             You can help me. I know everything about you.

GRIGORY You know what is on internet

HENRY   At your home Olympics in Moscow you won bronze in one
             hundred metres backstroke.

GRIGORY No Americans at Moscow. They made a boycott.

HENRY   A medal is a medal no?

GRIGORY You say this to Americans!
             But you're right.

                    □

             Anyway. Good luck.

                    □

             Please can you go.

HENRY   This is more important than my swimming. This country has
             many many problems.

GRIGORY I know.

HENRY   You don't.

GRIGORY My driver has a gun, I can see.

HENRY   But you don't understand.

GRIGORY Probably I do not.

HENRY   Probably you understand nothing.

GRIGORY Probably yes.
            But how I know there are problems?

HENRY   Internet.

GRIGORY Because no swim coach ever come to Congo. Only me.
            Madness job.
            Before, I am married, and my son he is love his father – I
            never come to Congo. Now, I am divorce and my son is angry
            and he live in England and throw his life in toilet. So I am
            okay to come to Congo. But is madness job. And the man I
            come for is like the slow Eric from Guinea?
            Eric the Eel.

HENRY   I'm not like him. I am a true swimmer.
            I am Lucky Henry.

GRIGORY You said this.

HENRY   You don't know my story.

GRIGORY I do actually. It's why they give you money, why they give me
            money.
            You were child soldier.

HENRY   No.

GRIGORY The money is not for your swimming my friend.

HENRY   I was not a child soldier.

                   □

GRIGORY Okay then, I don't know your story.

HENRY   No one knows it.

            But I will tell you because you are my Coach.

GRIGORY Don't tell me.

HENRY   I want to.

GRIGORY I don't want to know

HENRY   I want you to know Coach.

GRIGORY I'm not your Coach.

HENRY   My story is I am from the East. The East is war, always.
              I said I have escape from a rebel army.
              And then they give me good place in a commune. And then
              European charity they take me here to Kinshasa.

GRIGORY Okay.

HENRY   But I was never a child soldier. Really I am an orphan.

GRIGORY Why you say child soldier?

HENRY   The charity don't take orphans, only child soldiers.

GRIGORY Ah.

HENRY   A lot of us we say we are child soldiers.
              Some actually become child soldiers to join the charity.
              My friend Baptiste, he kill maybe twenty people while he wait
              to join the charity.
              He was very sad about this, but he got a good place in the
              commune.

                        □

GRIGORY Is difficult for you but I cannot help.

HENRY   One day I was looking for wood. When I return to my village
              everything is burned. My home is burned. My Father is
              burned.

GRIGORY You cannot have coach only because he is sad for you.

HENRY   Don't be sad for *me*, I did not die – I am Lucky Henry.

GRIGORY Go home Lucky Henry.

HENRY   When do you fly?

GRIGORY I fly soon.

HENRY   Tomorrow?

GRIGORY Yah soon.

HENRY   You book a ticket.

GRIGORY Yah, *soon*.

HENRY   Book soon or go soon?

                 ■

GRIGORY Henry I cannot talk now.

HENRY   I can help you book ticket Coach.

GRIGORY Is difficult.

HENRY   Is not difficult coach. Click click, finish.

GRIGORY Is difficult problem.

HENRY   Difficult how?

GRIGORY Difficult because.
     Because

HENRY   Because?

GRIGORY Because best price to Moscow, one thousand five hundred
     dollar.

          □

HENRY   Oh, you don't have money.

GRIGORY No I have money but

HENRY   You don't have money!

GRIGORY Is funny?

HENRY   Pardon me Coach but. Mundele [white man] always have
     money.

GRIGORY All my money, is in my home in Moscow.

HENRY   You forget your money?

GRIGORY The apartment *is* the money. Because I am sell but. The deal
     is. Not finish and. I have return ticket but eight weeks future.
     So, to fly, I am wait for money.

HENRY   From where?

GRIGORY I am ask my wife.

HENRY   New wife?
     You say you are divorce.

          ■

GRIGORY Ex-wife.

HENRY   In Congo we say: I have a cow in heaven but I cannot drink
     the milk.

GRIGORY Henry, please.

HENRY   Actually cows do not go in heaven. I think they just die.

GRIGORY Go home now.

HENRY   We also say, the hardest fly to kill is the one on your *(Points to his crotch.)*

   HENRY laughs, GRIGORY almost does.

        It will be a privilege for me to be coach by Grigory Polonsky for one day.
        One day of training, but first, my wife can cook for you.

        ■

GRIGORY Do you *forget* idea of London?

HENRY   Why Coach?

GRIGORY Because you will never qualify. You agree?

        ■

        Henry?

HENRY   Why Coach?

GRIGORY Maybe we can swim while I am / wait

HENRY   You train me!

GRIGORY Only while I am wait. And *only* if you forget idea of London – agree or I never coach you more

        ■

HENRY   I agree.

GRIGORY What you agree?

HENRY   I am not going to London. I will never qualify.

GRIGORY Stop smiling at me Henry.

HENRY   Okay I promise.

GRIGORY Good.

HENRY   I promise I won't qualify for the London Olympic games – how is that?

GRIGORY Good.

        Now you can enjoy your swimming.

I will make you best freestyle swimmer in Central Africa.

HENRY   Thank you Coach.

GRIGORY There are no good freestyle swimmers in Central Africa. So is probably easy.

5.

GRIGORY is eating Congolese food. HENRY is watching.

GRIGORY Very good.
Very good.
Your wife is very good chef.

HENRY   She is.

GRIGORY But actually there are many bones in this.

HENRY   Actually there are many bones in animals.

GRIGORY это правда. [That's true]
Yes, very very good food.
It's sad actually.

□

HENRY   Sad?

GRIGORY Of course you cannot eat this.

HENRY   Again?

GRIGORY Is not food for athlete.

HENRY   This is Congolese food, very healthy very good food.

HENRY takes a spoonful of food.

GRIGORY Very good food yes. Is not food for athlete.

GRIGORY takes the spoon.

GRIGORY I put you on diet.

GRIGORY eats it.

HENRY   What for?

GRIGORY We start with discipline, so when I am go, my discipline can stay.

HENRY   Are you a diet specialist?

GRIGORY Specialist? No. So maybe Congo Olympic Committee pay for diet specialist. But probably they don't, probably they have no fucking money. So probably I am your diet specialist. And I say, is not food for athlete.

HENRY   My wife will be angry with this.

GRIGORY Okay I speak with her.
Tell me about your job.

HENRY   I work for MONUSCO, the UN Mission in Congo.

GRIGORY Hours?

HENRY   From thirteen to twenty-one hours.

GRIGORY Physical work?

HENRY   I work in security but truly I walk around the perimeter of one building, many times. And I open the baggage of people to look for guns. And I watch women walking up and down.

GRIGORY So morning, evening, we train.

HENRY   There is a problem with morning.

GRIGORY Yes?

HENRY   I have English class, Kinshasa University, nine to eleven.

☐

GRIGORY I think not so important.

HENRY   Very important to me.

GRIGORY Why?

HENRY   For when I go to London.

GRIGORY How you go London?

HENRY   Swimming.

GRIGORY You cannot. I am only stay short time but. If I am stay long time, still never London.

HENRY   Who knows God's plan?

■

GRIGORY Okay Henry, you go English class in morning two days, train for three days in the week. And evenings. And Saturday. Yes?

HENRY   Yes Coach.

GRIGORY Also hotel swimming pool, not enough clean, not enough big

HENRY   Yes Coach.

GRIGORY Tomorrow is final day you train in this pool.

HENRY   In Kinshasa, we have a problem with the number and the size
of pools.

GRIGORY Where are best pools?

HENRY   Uh. The American School. And the Grand Hotel Kinshasa.

GRIGORY Okay I speak with them.

HENRY   But it is not possible to swim there.

GRIGORY I speak with them.
We will make revolution in your technique. Longer strokes,
more efficient.
Now, you want to show me something?

HENRY   DVD. Chariots of Fire.

GRIGORY It is long?

HENRY   Yes it is very long.

GRIGORY Ah shit.

HENRY   No it is beautiful.

Olympic athletes, they race not to win, but for God. Or to
change something.

GRIGORY Olympic athletes race always to win.

HENRY   Change a piece of the world. I want to change a piece / of the
world

GRIGORY Bullshit.

HENRY   Also it's good for your English.

■

GRIGORY My English is good.

HENRY   Your English is okay.

GRIGORY I teach myself.

HENRY   I know.

GRIGORY How you know?

HENRY   It is clear from how you speak.

GRIGORY I coach in English five years.

HENRY   Your coaching English better than your conversational
             English.

GRIGORY Who is this man I speak to, fucking. Charles Dickens?

HENRY   It's not important.

GRIGORY Thailand, Korea, everywhere I work, in English – very
             successful, I make less mistakes than you.

HENRY laughs.

             Yes?

HENRY   'Countable and uncountable nouns'. *Fewer* Mistakes.

GRIGORY Play your fucking DVD.
             Ten minutes only.

They are watching the DVD.

The Vangelis theme plays.

The lights go off suddenly and the Vangelis theme stops.

HENRY   Is electricity. Wait two minutes.

                    ☐

             Electricity stop many times. In your hotel it is okay they have
             a generator, but here. Problem.

                    ☐

GRIGORY Happen many times?

HENRY   Yeah, many times.
             This is why I must swim. So I can say to the world, This
             country, Congo, is full of troubles. Even the light it never
             works. We have no electricity but in the East, people they
             mine for mineral and die in wars, all because of electric
             company. Like Chariots of Fire, I can swim for something.
             At the Olympics, all the world will listen.

GRIGORY You will never go Olympics Henry!

HENRY   Even wildcard?

GRIGORY Forget wildcard, wildcard is politics. Never Olympics, understand?

HENRY I understand, sorry Coach.

■

The electricity returns, lights and music.

But ey, we are alive! We have electricity. We are going to the Olympics.

GRIGORY Henry you not go Olympics – turn this off one minute.

HENRY Coach, wait – it gets better.

GRIGORY To talk.

HENRY turns it off

This is why you swim? To change?

HENRY Yes Coach.

GRIGORY Swimming is about most possible fast.

HENRY Yes but

GRIGORY That is all. Most possible fast. For your body and your mind.

Nothing else. Understand?

HENRY I understand Coach.

The Vangelis theme rises up again.

A sequence begins. They are elsewhere.

GRIGORY First week: Freestyle swimming drills. Half time in pool, half time in classroom. Physics, theory, turns, starts, stroke rate. Second week: Everything in pool. We start at American school.

HENRY How?

GRIGORY produces a bronze medal.

Ah, magnifique.

GRIGORY I say – I want to get one of these for Congo.

HENRY You think I can win medal for Congo?

GRIGORY No. I say bullshit because we need new pool.

Right now, you try too hard, your stroke rate is too high.

GRIGORY hands HENRY a matchbox-sized device.

> This is for you.
> Is called Wetronome.

HENRY　Wet-ro-nome.

GRIGORY　Put it in your cap. For rhythm.
> You will be much faster.
> Beep. Stroke.
> Beep. Stroke.
> You are dog, I am Pavlov.
> Beep. Stroke.
> See?

A loud beep.

> From now, you never swim without Wetronome.

Another beep.

> Soon you hear in your brain even when you don't wear it.

A beep.

> You get a longer stroke, or maybe you go mad.

A beep.

> Maybe both.

A beep.

> Don't think just follow sound.

The beeps grow.

The Vangelis theme rises up.

The beeps grow. And subside. They are at the pool.

GRIGORY　Okay good work.

HENRY　How many?

GRIGORY　See you tomorrow.

HENRY　Coach?

GRIGORY　Don't eat your wife's food.

HENRY　I know I am getting faster.

GRIGORY　Stop asking about qualifying Henry.

HENRY   How many seconds away?

GRIGORY You are getting faster. That is all.

HENRY   Coach, how many?

GRIGORY You really want to know.

HENRY   Of course.

GRIGORY Today's time. Only one tenth of second short of qualifying time.

HENRY   Mon Dieu!

GRIGORY For women.
Six seconds short for men.

          ■

HENRY   I understand. I'm a joke.

          □

GRIGORY You much more fast now Henry. Is natural: you have longer stroke, you have new turn, more fitness, more rhythm.
But you are not Olympic athlete. You are a good man. Good swimmer.
But is impossible.

          □

Everyday I will write in chalk, your time. And you can look. But I not talk with you about *qualify for Olympics*.

HENRY   Thank you Coach. I will prove you wrong.

GRIGORY Go home. And stop smiling.

The beeps begin again, insistent.

Music rises up.

GRIGORY begins to write on the chalkboard.

Times written at intervals. Getting remarkably quicker.

A sequence, in the style of a montage in a sporting underdog movie – the convention being beeps, music and chalked-up times create a sense of momentum.

HENRY   I was very fast today.

GRIGORY You are work very hard.

HENRY   I enjoy training

GRIGORY Your improvement is special. Congratulations.

HENRY   You speak with your wife? Ex-wife.

GRIGORY Yes it is.
            It is take time.

■

HENRY   I want to have a chance at qualifying.

GRIGORY You don't have it.

HENRY   With God's help, I will qualify.

GRIGORY Miracle, yah.

HENRY   He made me to race. I believe that God made me for a
            purpose. When I swim, I feel his pleasure.

GRIGORY Stop it.

HENRY   To swim is to honour him.

GRIGORY Please stop saying words from Chariot of Fire.

□

HENRY   I also believe them.

■

            I know what I need to qualify

GRIGORY Yah, you need to swim the fucking time. At official FINA
            swimming meet. Which is impossible.

HENRY   I can hit the time.

GRIGORY I don't believe you can hit the time. But more: there are no
            meets for you.

    HENRY has details on paper.

HENRY   Qualification from le Fédération Internationale de Natation
            finish on the third of July. There's only three qualifying events
            in Africa before. Two of them are national meets, only open
            to swimmers from that country. So I cannot enter. But one
            in Durban South Africa, has been approved as an Olympic
            qualifier by FINA.

GRIGORY I know.

HENRY   International invitation meet, Durban. In ten days. And I think I can have funding to go to this, from an NGO.

GRIGORY There's a problem with that Henry.

HENRY   They *want* me to have the money.

GRIGORY Another problem.

HENRY   How?

GRIGORY The problem with the invitational event

HENRY   Yes

GRIGORY Is you must be invite.

■

HENRY   So they must invite me.

GRIGORY They not invite you.

HENRY   They must.

GRIGORY They do not invite you. I try one month ago.

HENRY   You tried.

GRIGORY It was not possible.
            They need all space for other Africans. Congo Olympic Committee is not important. And no money for bribe.

□

HENRY   Thank you for your attempt, Coach.
            You believed.

GRIGORY I believe you never fucking stop talking about qualification.

HENRY   Thanks Coach.

   The beeps rise and subside.

   GRIGORY and HENRY are back watching the DVD.

   Music playing.

   Maybe both of them are crying, or moved.

GRIGORY You're right, better third time watching.

HENRY   Tomorrow, I will know about the wildcard.

GRIGORY Stop.

> Stop your dream. You not go Olympics.
> But you are one athlete who change. Against my prediction.
> You become competitive swimmer.

HENRY   Thank you Coach.

GRIGORY I try wildcards in many countries, it is hell, it is politics.

HENRY   I understand.

GRIGORY You will never have wildcard.

HENRY   Okay Coach. But I am Lucky Henry.

HENRY smiles.

6.

Classroom. HENRY stands with a sheet of paper.

HENRY   Professor Mbangwe, for my Technical reading, I have one new
piece of English to read to the class.

> It is from a website of the International Olympic Committee.

He beams and nods.

> 'In order to gain maximum participation at the Twenty
> Twelve London Olympics, the Democratic Republic of
> Congo requested wild-card entries to the wrestling, athletics
> and swimming events. They have been granted two, Joseph
> Kiyake in the eight hundred metres athletics.
> And former child-soldier Henry Kompolo Lumbwi in the one
> hundred metres Freestyle swimming.'

HENRY beams and bows to the class.

> Thank you.
> I will be speaking English I learn from this class, in London!
> I use my English to tell them of the problems here.

7.

GRIGORY's hotel room.

GRIGORY has opened a bottle of vodka.

GRIGORY He was a very good child. Very quiet. His nature, so calm.

☐

Then.

■

I don't know.

HENRY   I know you are a good father.

GRIGORY pours them a vodka.

GRIGORY   You miss your father?

HENRY   This is good for my training?

GRIGORY   It's the best. Good vodka: never headache next day.
                        За Дружба между народами.
                        To friendship between nations

HENRY   Friendship between nations.

They drink.

                        In the morning we go early tomorrow to airport because with
                        a white man, they will want big bribes.

GRIGORY   Yah yah, I know.

HENRY   I have never been to Europe. In Congo we say Poto.
                        Even without the Olympics. To go to Poto, is a dream for me.

GRIGORY   Is not so special.

HENRY   Ha. You are happy to go back to Poto?

GRIGORY   Back?

HENRY   Yes.

GRIGORY   I am not European.

HENRY   You are.

GRIGORY   Like you say – au contraire.

HENRY   Russia play football in Europe.

GRIGORY   Russia do many things in Europe. We are never European.

HENRY   You are Asian?

GRIGORY   No, we're Russian. Is different.

HENRY   Do the people where we are going, they like Russia?

GRIGORY   British people, uh no. I think no.

HENRY   British people like Congo?

GRIGORY I dunno Henry, you think I know fucking everything British? My son live there, I don't talk to him. Probably they don't know Congo.

But, one thing is good for you. British people love underdog.

□

HENRY   Explain underdog?

GRIGORY It's the person or team in the low position.

HENRY   Okay.

GRIGORY With no chance, they have big disadvantage. I think British people will support Lucky Henry.

HENRY   Ha. I hope it's true.

□

Also this country is *underdog*.
Congo is underdog.

GRIGORY Yah, but.
It's not sport.

HENRY   Okay.

GRIGORY Only underdog in sport really.

HENRY   Okay.

HENRY smiles.

GRIGORY What is it?

HENRY   It's too important. They must listen. About our problems here.

■

GRIGORY Promise me. You are not disappoint when people do not listen.

HENRY smiles. GRIGORY pours another.

To a swimmer who has beaten all of my prediction.

HENRY   To a coach who changed / my life

GRIGORY No no, you wait!

HENRY   Sorry.

GRIGORY Next time. Is my toast, you toast next time

HENRY   Sorry Coach.

GRIGORY Is kind, but.
                Okay go, say.

HENRY   Say?

GRIGORY You can say.

HENRY   Say what?

GRIGORY The toast about.
                Okay don't.

HENRY   Now?
                To a / coach

GRIGORY No stop, enough enough.

                    □

HENRY   You are sad.

GRIGORY I'm not.

HENRY   You never smile.

GRIGORY In London. I will smile. A deal for you.

HENRY   Deal Coach.

GRIGORY To The Olympic Games.

HENRY   The Olympic Games!

They drink another.

8.

Olympic Village, London. GRIGORY is massaging HENRY's back.

HENRY is drinking a big glass of water with a straw.

HENRY   Who else?

GRIGORY Michael Klim.
                Maria Sharapova.
                Mark Foster.
                Anastasia Grishina. Russian gymnastic, you don't know, very
                cute actually.
                Uh, Pele.

HENRY   You see Pele?

GRIGORY Yah.

HENRY   What was he doing?

GRIGORY He was uh, he was outside village, talk to TV.

HENRY   It is very funny they call this a village.
Really this is not a village.
This not like any village I ever see.
Is this like any village in Russia?

GRIGORY No.

HENRY   It's magnifique.

GRIGORY giggles.

GRIGORY Is fucking amazing actually.

HENRY   It is fucking amazing Coach. Pardonnez moi.
Who else you see?

GRIGORY And of course I see Popov.

HENRY   Popov?

GRIGORY Stop moving.

HENRY   Sorry.

GRIGORY I show you Popov, on Youtube, he is Russian freestyle one
hundred metres, fifty metres – *genius of pool.*

HENRY   Oh Popov.

GRIGORY Yah I see Popov in Westfield. He was eat sushi.

HENRY   You know Popov from before I think.

GRIGORY Uh, little.

HENRY   You say hello?

GRIGORY Uh. Yes I say hello. Who you see?

HENRY   What did Popov say?

GRIGORY He think I am someone different.

HENRY   Oh

GRIGORY Is okay. No problem. Who you see?

HENRY   I saw Bolt.

GRIGORY You see Bolt!

HENRY I saw Bolt in the village, walking away in a big crowd. And I think I saw Beckham but. Many mundele look like Beckham.

GRIGORY Where you see Beckham?

HENRY He was driving a bus.

GRIGORY Then probably is not Beckham.

They laugh.

HENRY No, probably is not Beckham.

☐

GRIGORY Henry you are tight

HENRY I am very relaxed

GRIGORY Your heart is very fast

HENRY My heart is always very fast

GRIGORY No heart is *always* fast

HENRY Mine is

GRIGORY You are too excite

HENRY You are *more* excited

GRIGORY Me?

HENRY You are too excited.

GRIGORY No no, this is normal for me. Is your first Olympics

HENRY You are *not* excited Coach?

GRIGORY Henry, this is job for me.
Very good to be at Olympics for sure, but is only job.

HENRY Let me feel your heart.

GRIGORY Don't touch my heart.

Henry

HENRY Oh no! I cannot feel anything.

GRIGORY Fucking lie down.

HENRY Do you have a heart Coach?

GRIGORY Too much excite.

HENRY I am worried you are born without a heart. The heart is very important.

GRIGORY Lie down.

HENRY This water is delicious.

GRIGORY After training today, I want you to sleep.

HENRY Unfortunately not possible.

GRIGORY Why?

HENRY After training I have to meet a top journalist, from 'Associated Press'.

GRIGORY Ah *of course.*

HENRY You know them?

GRIGORY You are not funny Henry.

HENRY And other journalists also. To ask me about the problems of Congo.

GRIGORY Be serious.

HENRY It's true.

HENRY has finished his water and is going to refill.

Would you like water?

GRIGORY I want you to sleep and also you drink too much water.

HENRY Oh.
But it's free.

GRIGORY Yes I know.

HENRY It's kitchen water. From tap.

GRIGORY Yes I know.

HENRY Ah, do they make us pay when we leave?

GRIGORY No, it's free Henry, but is possible you drink too much water.

HENRY Truly?

GRIGORY In Congo you have no easy water, now you have easy water, you drink too much.

HENRY What is for lunch today Coach?

GRIGORY Fish – protein.

HENRY And it is possible I can meet your son?

■

GRIGORY Probably.

HENRY It is possible *you* can meet your son?

GRIGORY Tomorrow. I meet him tomorrow.

HENRY Great news.

□

GRIGORY Yah, I hope. Okay, let's look at heat times. To see your competition

HENRY Many good swimmers.

GRIGORY Show me. Which swimmers you have?

HENRY Voila.

HENRY gives him a card.

GRIGORY Okay.

Good competition, make you swim more fast. New Personal best.

And

черт! [Devil]

Shit fuck Africa.

HENRY What's wrong Coach?

GRIGORY Again!

HENRY Again what?

GRIGORY I am in England one day and still your country has problem for me.

GRIGORY shows him the card.

Explain please.

HENRY That's my name.

HENRY laughs.

Oh Mon Dieu, that is bad.

GRIGORY Is funny?

HENRY   That's a bad error.

GRIGORY Ten seconds too long.

HENRY   Maybe they use the time from two months ago.

GRIGORY Your time, for the Olympic heat, they write ten seconds too long. Who are people write this?

HENRY   They are politicians, they are friends of the President, not sport people.

GRIGORY Well this very fucked.

HENRY   In Congo we have this always. Administration is not our best skill.

GRIGORY I coach one athlete, very rare. Normally I coach maybe four. My final Olympics, one athlete. You. And you *will swim* personal best.

      □

HENRY   With this time, I definitely will.

GRIGORY But the time false!
I retire. Right now, I retire.

HENRY   Don't retire Coach.

GRIGORY Too late. I retire

HENRY   Please don't retire.

GRIGORY I conjugate verb to retire. I retire, I retired, I am retired, I have retired.

HENRY   Please stop retiring Coach.

GRIGORY Is not funny.

HENRY   I see you are worried to meet your son.

GRIGORY It not about my son.

HENRY   Okay Coach.

      □

      ■

GRIGORY When you say you meet journalists

HENRY   Yes Coach.

GRIGORY That is joke.

HENRY No. That is true

GRIGORY *This* why they want to meet. They see your slow time, they think you are new Eric Eel Catastrophe.

HENRY They come to listen about Congo.

GRIGORY They don't. And we must change time.

HENRY You say journalists only want to listen because of my slow Pee Bee.

GRIGORY Sorry but. Yes.

HENRY Is not right.

GRIGORY No not right but

HENRY So if we change time, maybe they will not listen?

GRIGORY Henry

HENRY And not listen to the problems.

GRIGORY No Henry.

HENRY So maybe we leave the time

GRIGORY Maybe I punch your face.

HENRY Leave the time and all the world listen to Lucky Henry.

GRIGORY No one will listen.

HENRY And I will help my country.

GRIGORY You will do nothing.

HENRY God put me in the Olympics for a reason.

GRIGORY I put you in fucking Olympics.

HENRY Grigory you change my life. But I am here because I have Wildcard. Not because of you. That Wildcard was given to me by God.
My life was saved for me in East Congo by Jesus.
If I come here and swim and I *don't* tell people about the problems, I will be a failure. If I don't speak about my country, I am a failure even if I win the *gold medal.*

GRIGORY You cannot win gold medal.

HENRY   It is not because of you the time is wrong. It is just a mistake.
           All you have to do. Is nothing.
           Just nothing.

           ■

GRIGORY   But this Pee Bee time is joke.
           You are not joke Henry. I am not *joke*.

HENRY   But if my best time is bad and you are my coach. You not will
           look a joke.
           You will look like you make a miracle.

           ■

           Maybe your son see a miracle?

           □

           Leave the Pee Bee Coach? And make a miracle. And I can
           talk about my country

GRIGORY   Ah, this is very fucked.
           I leave false Pee Bee.
           But no one will listen.

HENRY   Thank you Coach! You do a good thing for my country.

9.

HENRY is giving an interview.

HENRY   Ey, thank you, many people. Wow.
           Thank you. No. No translation please.
           I am fluent in Swahili, Lingala, French and English.
           My name is Lucky Henry. When people ask Why are you
           called Lucky Henry? I say, It's because I have survived many
           horrors. God has saved me and every time in my life I make
           the best of the situation.
           You know, I am very proud to swim for Congo because there
           are so many problems there. And really the world does not
           understand I think.
           We have always had war, for fifteen years. And it is because
           of minerals for computers that everyone uses. Many electrics

companies make money from these minerals, maybe some
sponsors of this Olympic games make money from these
minerals. It's very important that people listen.
Yes?
No I don't know him.
No I have never met Eric the Eel.
But I know he is here as coach for Guinea. He has a good life.
We could swim together maybe!
Ha.
Yes?
Of course I am confident, I am Lucky Henry.

He beams.

10.

Village. GRIGORY is showing HENRY a smartphone.

GRIGORY Calendar, diary, email, internet, instant message.
This is apps.
Apps I am not actually understand.
High-res screen, camera – video and photo. Big memory.
Torch.

HENRY   Torch?

GRIGORY turns the torch on.

GRIGORY Torch.

Turns the torch off.

HENRY   I think it is better to have a torch.

GRIGORY For sure, but. When you don't have torch:

GRIGORY turns the torch on again.

Yah?

Turns torch off. Sees at the time on the phone.

Soon I must go for lunch.

HENRY   What is lunch today Grigory?

GRIGORY Today I am eat with my son. Sasha. And his girl.

HENRY   Magnifique.

GRIGORY lets HENRY take the smartphone to look at it.

GRIGORY Good interview?

HENRY   Long.

GRIGORY That's good. They are interest.

HENRY   Yes.

GRIGORY They ask about uh. About me?

HENRY   They asked me about Eric the Eel.

GRIGORY And you say?

HENRY   I said I do not know him.
An American said Eric is always travelling now, last year he swam in Japan for two months. And USA. He works for oil company and.
Why is your phone in English language?

GRIGORY Sasha give me in English. For learning.

HENRY   Kind.

GRIGORY Yah. Actually.
Very kind. He uh.
He is man now.
I think he is happy.

HENRY beams, and gives the phone back.

HENRY   I am truly pleased for you Coach.

HENRY looks to leave the room.

GRIGORY He give me phone. I give him ticket for pool tomorrow.
He is not going to work, he is coming to pool, to watch us.

HENRY is agitatedly trying to leave.

HENRY   Perfect.

GRIGORY Henry where are you go?

                    □

HENRY   To look out of the window.

GRIGORY Henry are you go to the toilet again?

                    ∎

Henry, I tell you.

HENRY   Sorry Coach.

GRIGORY Stop drink fucking water Henry. Stop you will drown in this
water.

HENRY   It's very beautiful water.

GRIGORY Over-hydration.

HENRY   Okay sorry.

GRIGORY Okay.

HENRY   Okay.
This is hurting now.

GRIGORY Go.

HENRY leaves.

☐

GRIGORY checks his smartphone.

☐

☐

Interview!
Interview Henry!
Sasha email your interview.

HENRY runs in doing up his trousers.

HENRY   Interview!

GRIGORY Sasha say is good interview.

HENRY   Okay magnifique.

GRIGORY He say it is everywhere on the web.

HENRY   I can see?

GRIGORY He say – ah. Его российской письменной плохо сейчас. [His
written Russian is bad now]

HENRY   Show me Coach

GRIGORY His Russian very bad now.

HENRY   Coach show me?

GRIGORY Too long England.

HENRY   Read it Coach.

GRIGORY You read, your English uh,
                My eyes hurt reading screen.

HENRY reads.

HENRY   'Could Lucky Henry Lumbwi be this Olympics' Loveable
                Loser?
                The Democratic Republic of Congo has never won an
                Olympic medal in its history, and swimmer Henry Lumbwi
                seems unlikely to break that duck.'

GRIGORY What duck?

HENRY   Duck?

GRIGORY What you do to duck?

HENRY   I never say anything about duck.

GRIGORY Very strange.

HENRY   'Christened Lucky Henry by a Belgian Missionary, Lumbwi'

GRIGORY Chris – what

HENRY   Name – he give me name.

GRIGORY Belgian Missionary, is true?

HENRY   Uh. I can't remember.

GRIGORY You can't remember is true!

HENRY   I say it many times but. I *think* it's true, I cannot remember.
                'Lumbwi seems fully re-ha-bili-tated
                 from his early life as a child soldier
                in a brutal East African jungle war.'
                Nothing of Congo!

GRIGORY Yah it say first line, Congo Olympic Swimmer

HENRY   Nothing of problems.

GRIGORY He is not journalist of Africa.

HENRY   I tell about the problems for twenty minutes.

GRIGORY Read more.

HENRY 'His coach Grigory Polonsky, himself a backstroke bronze for the USSR at the wide-ly boycott-ed Moscow Olympics, was'

GRIGORY черт [Devil], always fucking boycott.

HENRY 'was found through an international programme matching coaches with athletes from de-veloping countries.
Lucky Henry's story is the stuff Olympic dreams are made of. Another re-cip-ient of the IOC wildcard system, he claims Sydney's hero Eric the Eel is an inspiration to him.' Qua!

GRIGORY You say this!

HENRY I say Eric Eel has a very good life.

GRIGORY Inspiration?

HENRY   'However he swims tomorrow – and his official time suggests the other swimmers could be dry when he finally touches home – Lucky Henry may just find himself in the affection of Londoners for a long time to come.'

□

Nothing. I talk about problems for twenty minutes.

GRIGORY You know all this men are journalist for sport?

HENRY Of course.

GRIGORY They cannot write front page London Times, Congo is very fucked.
Don't be disappoint.

HENRY It doesn't matter I swim fast or swim slow, no body listen.

GRIGORY Ah Henry I tell you. Don't be disappoint. You are famous.

HENRY Maybe the true way to a good life is come to Poto Olympics and swim slow.

GRIGORY Henry this is chemical reaction in your brain. Today, you feel low only because before you are high. Before I am say – you are too much excite. You walk in Olympic village trying the high five for everybody, breathing so fast. I say Calm calm Henry. True?

HENRY True.

GRIGORY You have big swim tomorrow. Nerves, strange thinking, very normal.

Near your dream, suddenly the question come – what it
mean?
Maybe my dream is only worth shit.
But I say, is worth very much.

■

Maybe rest, or enjoy the village. I must go lunch with my Son.
I am late actually.

GRIGORY is leaving.

HENRY   Coach?

GRIGORY Yes.

HENRY   ■

GRIGORY I late!

HENRY   Okay bon appétit.

■

GRIGORY You only have nerves. Tomorrow I come to you before race.
              And I will have something to say.
              I will uh,
              find some
              Words.
              Before you swim.

11.

HENRY is in his swimsuit. Nervous.

GRIGORY enters behind him.

GRIGORY Ah.

HENRY   Hey Grigory.

■

GRIGORY Sleep was good?

HENRY   Very good.

GRIGORY I did not sleep.

■

Henry I think I love this phone.
Yesterday I give Google one question.
In history of Olympics, what number swimmers is ten seconds faster than Pee Bee?

☐

Do you know?

HENRY   No Grigory.

GRIGORY Make guess.

HENRY   I am sorry Grigory, I don't know

GRIGORY Okay, I tell you.
None. Zero.
Never.
Never before today
Before I not think this is right way but.

☐

We know each other now Henry.
I am at lunch yesterday, and I think – I know you more than my son.
We know each other very close.
We know life is difficult.
We know we cannot win medal.
We know the world is not Chariot of Fire.
But we know we can win something.
We can win some little history.
Some little
Some little *corner*
Of history.
For us.

■

You don't swim alone today Henry.
You swim with Congo, and you swim with God, and you swim with me.
Bonne chance.

■

HENRY   Thank you Grigory. Thank you for everything.

12.

GRIGORY is about to watch the Olympic heat. He kneads his hands.
The beeper sounds.

GRIGORY давай! [Come on] давай Henry!

Fucking move Henry!

Ты ведь умеешь! [You can make it]

Come on!

☐

дав

GRIGORY stares.

☐

☐

■

☐

GRIGORY folds his arms and looks away.

■

■

He looks back.

He shakes his head.

And looks away.

HENRY emerges from the water.

He passes GRIGORY walking away.

In front of a board of sponsors' logos, HENRY is interviewed.

HENRY   Thank you. No. No translation please.

I am fluent in Swahili, Lingala, French and English.

My name is Lucky Henry.

God has saved me and every time in my life I make the best of the situation. The most important thing in the Olympic Games is not winning but taking part. That is the Olympic creed, Pierre de Coubertin, very beautiful.

And I swim today, because I love to take part. And I think I
beat my Personal Best today by, yes by one second. So.
I hope with God's help I can keep meeting people and
travelling the world and keep swimming. I love being in the
water, the water is for me like a second skin, my wife will tell
you I love being in the water almost as much as being in her
arms. Actually sometimes more but I can't say this to her!
Sorry again?
For me today is about swimming and sport and taking part,
and I don't have anything to say really about this.
You know the problems of my country are hard for me to
understand, so of course *very* hard for other people.
So I have to leave this to the politicians, but of course I swim
for peace.

13.

Village. HENRY in his room, on the phone.

HENRY   Okay.
              Thank you.

    A roar of anger from outside.

              Yes I feel okay.
              I talked with my wife, she is looking forward to meeting you
              one day soon. I would like for her to fly here very soon.
              Is possible? Magnifique.
              Sponsor for me?
              Yes okay.
              Maybe, I am thinking, we can make a film. Of my story.
              I go back to Congo, the cameras see the problems.
              Okay we can talk. I will see you in one hour.

    A roar from outside.

              Can we meet in the Athletes' centre? Not here.
              Because my coach is shouting outside my room.
              Yes that was him.

    He laughs.

              He is actually really nice.

No, no security, we can talk.

Okay thank you.

HENRY finishes the call.

Another roar from outside.

Please Grigory.

GRIGORY Open door Henry

Fu

☐

HENRY Please Grigory, come back when you are not drunk.

GRIGORY Open the fucking door.

черт!

☐

I will wait fucking all day.

HENRY Tomorrow when you are sober. I will explain.

GRIGORY Open fucking door Henry. I am still your coach.

Open this fucking door.

HENRY lets him in warily, GRIGORY stumbles a little.

■

When you get agent?

HENRY Have some water.

GRIGORY When you get agent Henry?

HENRY About twenty minutes ago, you want water?

GRIGORY Fuck your water from tap

HENRY Please Grigory. I break the Pee Bee!

GRIGORY Pee Bee is false. False time is submit by you?

Fucking yes?

HENRY Grigory do you ever think you swear too much?

■

GRIGORY You are disgrace. You not swim most possible fast. For your

body and mind.

My son, he is very high in the stadium, to watch your *miracle*.

HENRY   You know why I swim slow.

GRIGORY I don't.

HENRY   You live with me in Congo.

GRIGORY And fucking what?

HENRY   Are you stupid Grigory?
Are you stupid?

GRIGORY Yah today I think I am, to be your friend I must be stupid

HENRY   At the moment, electricity is on in my life, bright electricity.
But after this Olympics, the electricity is off. Forever. You
lived with me there, you understand. Once the crow he taste
the honey, he cannot be happy with seeds.

GRIGORY I say to my son, this time is smashed today. Before I hope he
is proud, now I look like a piece of shit. You are happy with
that?
I look like catastrophe piece of shit to my son.

HENRY   You don't, he is happy to see you. He *has* a father.

GRIGORY You are fucking disgrace

GRIGORY makes a move to push HENRY and stumbles. GRIGORY is on the floor.

HENRY   I love my home, I love Congo but, I cannot *live* there. We
have to make the best. The crow he taste the honey.
I thought you understand.
I have sponsors wanting to talk. Many sponsors. For you also
maybe.

GRIGORY This is *very* fucked.

HENRY   If no one listen, I take for myself and make the best Grigory.

GRIGORY Call me coach
Call me coach Henry.

☐

Henry call me coach.

HENRY   You are not my coach, Grigory, I am sorry.
Do you, is it possible for you to understand?

■

GRIGORY is lying, drunk and beaten.

Grigory, please drink some water.

GRIGORY Call me Coach!

HENRY   Okay.
Coach.
Drink water with me.

GRIGORY Water from tap huh?

HENRY   Yes.

GRIGORY *Water from tap.*

HENRY   Yes.

HENRY hands GRIGORY a glass of water.

GRIGORY drinks the water in one.

End of play.

AFTER THE PARTY

I would like to thank Sam Hodges, Justin Cartwright
and Conrad Williams for reading early drafts of the script,
and for their many intelligent suggestions.

I'm also grateful to DJ Semtek, DJ Sabre, MC Stylistic G,
Swampy, Edi Drums and MC Shiznit for helping me
to cast my mind back to the heyday of UK Garage.

I dedicate this play to Anya and our son, Isaac.

The audio elements which are interspersed between

the scenes come in very quickly after the blackout of the

preceding scene. When the audio is over,

we return rapidly to the on-stage action.

SCENE 1

SEAN stands in a spotlight behind some decks on a podium in a club. A strobe effect. He is playing a UK Garage hit. The intense focus of a man at the top of his game, playing to thousands of people.

SEAN   So, how you feeling now Ayia Napa? Sexy ladies, the men looking dapper. This one's going out to the raving crews, hear the news: DJ Slinky on the ones-and-twos, shout to Sting-Ray the MC, looking liv-er-ly, we're doing it for us, we're doing it for you, people jump inside the venue.

SEAN's heavily pregnant girlfriend, CHELLE, enters and the lighting shifts to reveal a room in a shabby flat in Stratford, right next to the Olympic site. What looked like a podium is in fact a cheap table. We can now see that SEAN is wearing a baggy T-shirt and Y-fronts. We can now only just make out the tinny beat of the music through the headphones which are on SEAN's head.

CHELLE   Sean.

SEAN cannot hear her.

SEAN   When I say Ayia, you say Napa: Ayia… *(As though this is thousands of clubbers responding.)* Napa. I can't hear you…when I say Ayia, you say Napa: Ayia…

CHELLE   Sean, I'm leaving you.

SEAN sees her now for the first time, although he still hasn't heard her.

SEAN   Going out to the one-like Chelle, Bun in the oven but still tres belle,
Tasty and sweet like a creme caramelle,
She's my hot mademoiselle.
So, take that French GCSE, you was wrong to award me a fucking G,
And Madame Wiggins, are you listening…

CHELLE walks over to the decks just before the last line of SEAN's rap. She picks up the microphone, switches it on and shouts into it interrupting.

CHELLE   Sean, I'm leaving you!

SEAN tears the headphones from his head and cups his ears.

SEAN   Jesus, Chelle, what you do that for? Aghhh, I can't hear nothing. *(Beat.)* Oh my god, I'm deaf, you've deafened me.

CHELLE   Oh my God. Sean, can you hear me?

SEAN   I can't hear nothing. It's my ear drums. You've…my fucking
            ear drums. *(Pause.)* I think the ringing… I think the ringing
            is… I think, yes, it's… I think it's going. Say something, will
            you? *(Pause as CHELLE considers what to say.)* Just say anything.
            Whatever you was gonna say when you come in here.

CHELLE   I'm leaving you.

SEAN   Oh, thank God! Thank Christ that's over.

CHELLE   I'm really leaving you, Sean. I'm moving into Natalie's.

SEAN   What?

CHELLE   Says in my book that a partner who is failing to live up to his
            responsibilities is more a hindrance than a help and must be
            told to shape up or ship out. I can't tell you to ship out of your
            own flat, so I'm leaving.

SEAN   I don't get no warning?

CHELLE   *(Pointing to stomach.)* What doyou call this? Eight months,
            Sean. Eight months I've been telling you I want to get out. I
            told you in February about the new flats – Chobham Manor. I
            gave you the form for the shared ownership thing. We coulda
            had our name down by now. All we needed was a couple of
            grand to secure it but you done nothing.

SEAN   I'll look into it.

CHELLE   Iss too late, Sean! The deadline's in two weeks.

SEAN   Yeah but I've been busy. I got this set coming up at Mirage
            Club in Leyton. Iss a new night called Code Red. Old-school
            garage is back, babe. Norris da Boss Windross played there a
            couple of weeks ago.

CHELLE   So you're booked to play are you?

SEAN   Yes.

CHELLE   Who you playing with?

SEAN   Just me.

CHELLE   Ray's not involved then?

SEAN   Ray? No! Hardly see him these days, we kinda gone our
            separate ways, you know, drifted apart.

CHELLE   Interesting.

SEAN   Yeah, iss good opportunity, I mean, if Norris da Boss
              Windross has played there then…

CHELLE   Iss interesting because I just ran into Ray's mum and she said
              you was upstairs at his place last night playing X Box. She also
              said you was playing a set with him at a new garage night at
              Mirage Club in Leyton. *(Pause.)* So is she lying then? Look at
              me and tell me she's lying.

SEAN   OK, I'm playing with Ray but iss different this time, there's
              a booking agent gonna be there and there's a lot of interest
              suddenly.

CHELLE   Sean, please. Wake up! The only interest anyone has in you
              and Ray is working out what you're still doing banging around
              with that retard. Thass why we need to get out of the block.
              You got to get away from him, Sean. Even after everything
              he's done to you, iss like you're walking around with this big
              fat albatross hanging round your neck and you don't even
              know it's there. Wass it gonna be, Sean, me or Ray?

CHELLE starts to walk out.

SEAN   Iss not like that, babe. This could really sort us out. If we get
              snapped up by this booking agent, we could…

CHELLE   Too late. If you don't do something soon it'll be just you and
              Ray sat pissed down the Carpenters telling anyone who'll
              listen about what might have been all those years ago.

SEAN   Well it won't be The Carpenters – closing down on Thursday.
              I told them you'd be there. What will I say?

CHELLE   Tell em the truth: we broke up.

CHELLE walks to the door. SEAN follows.

SEAN   Don't go, Chelle. Natalie's gonna drive you mad in two
              minutes. Stay here and less talk it over. We're great together.

CHELLE exits.

Blackout.

DAVID CAMERON (V.O.)

>   Britain remains a great power.
>   I reject this idea that Britain is embarked on an inevitable path
>   of decline, that the rise of new powers is the end of Britain's
>   influence. The Olympic Games are about Great Britain, letting
>   the whole world see all that is great about our country – our
>   history, our present, our future. I believe this can be a great
>   advertisement for our country.

SCENE 2

The lights come up to reveal SEAN in a car park outside a rundown block of flats.
He is waiting nervously close to a very large object which is covered in a tarpaulin.
RAY, almost 30, enters immediately. His belly is practically bursting out of an
early noughties West Ham shirt, which bears the name "Di Canio" at the top
and beneath that "10" and beneath that "GOD". On his head is a pink crown of
modelling balloons in the shape of an animal.

RAY	Alright geez!
SEAN	Where you been? Oi, what the fuck is that?
RAY	Peppa Pig.
SEAN	No, wass is it doing on your head?
RAY	There's this geezer on stilts dressed as Wenlock and he's makin 'em for people. Iss completely free. Opening ceremony's not til tomorrow and iss all happening already. Mad, innit? How do I look?
SEAN	You look quite cool actually.
RAY	Really?
SEAN	You look like a fucking moron.
RAY	Don't care. Iss all part of a wider strategy, innit? You seen how many gorgeous birds there are just bowling round the manor? It's gonna be like shooting ducks in a barrel geez. First you've got to get 'em to clock you. It don't matter what it is. Could be anything – your hair, your physique, your…point is, the more

eye-catching, the better. You just want as many as possible to look, know you're there. That's Phase One – groundbait.

SEAN   So, they clock you and then what do you do?

RAY   Just give them a look. Something like this.

RAY arches his eyebrows creepily.

SEAN   Jesus, don't do that, geez.

RAY   You give em the look and thass it – feet up, beer, zoot – wait for them to come to you. And thass when you transition to Phase Two.

SEAN   Oh sure. Phase Two.

RAY   Take the piss all you want but when I'm in Phase Two, you'll know about it.

SEAN   Whatever you say, Ray. *(Pause.)* You weren't at your flat, where you been? Listen, need you to…

RAY   Oh, geez, I haven't told you about renting my flat out, have I?

SEAN   Geez, I wanna ask you something…

RAY   *(Interrupting.)* They come round bang on time right at 10. German couple. She's this big blonde bird, and he's got a skinhead. They seem nice enough, I show 'em in: lounge, sofabed and I go to tidy up the kitchen a bit and before I know it she's got her bloody kit off.

SEAN   Howdyou know?

RAY   I'm staring at her.

SEAN   She's just walking around in the nud?
RAY   Pretty much.

SEAN   Either she's walking around starkers or she ain't.

RAY   Well, she didn't close the door to the lounge.

SEAN   So, she just left it wide open?

RAY   Yeah…well, not wide open.

SEAN   Mainly closed or mainly open?

RAY   Wass it matter?

SEAN   You're a sick man.

RAY   Point is, Sean, she's just whipped her kit off and she's standing there right in front of me. And then she turns around and boom, right there on her arse guess what I seen, clear as day?

SEAN   Peppa Pig?

RAY   Two fucking swastikas.

SEAN   Don't believe ya.

RAY   Why would I make it up? I've rented my flat to bloody Nazis, mate, nudist Nazis.

SEAN   So what did you say?

RAY   Say? What was I supposed to say? Excuse me, you'll have to get out? Don't you watch the History Channel? If there's one lesson we've learned, geez, iss that Nazis do not like being told to get out. So I ain't gonna say nothing, geez. Words for show, actions for a pro.

SEAN   What? What does that mean?

RAY   One word: boobytraps. *(Beat.)* Don't worry, so long as they stick to their designated areas, don't start invading my space – mainly the coffee jar in the kitchen and the sock drawer in my bedroom, they'll be fine.

SEAN   What will they want in your sock drawer?

RAY   What did they want in Belgium? *(Beat.)* Anyway, they've paid the money at least and I spose 300 quid's 300 quid, innit?

SEAN   Howdyou fancy making a lot more? *(SEAN whips the tarpaulin off the object centre stage to reveal a triangular advertising trailer which has been badly converted into a catering van. The painted sign at the top reads "Albion Burgers". A large ill-fitting metal flap, which has clearly been salvaged from some other vehicle, covers the serving hatch/window.)* Paint still needs a bit of work.

RAY   What do you want with that heap of shit? You won't get much for it.

SEAN   Get much? I've bought it.

RAY   Bought it for what?

SEAN goes to the van, opens the door and goes inside. From there he gingerly opens the flap at the front to reveal a large hole which has been cut in the side of the trailer as a serving hatch. The sides are not straight.

SEAN   Gently does it. Albion, the geezer who sold it to me, said you gotta be careful doing this. He's just redone all the welding. *(SEAN gets the flap up and safely secured.)* Burgers, hotdogs and souvenirs. Whatdoyou reckon?

RAY   Where you gonna park it?

SEAN   Right here, geez. Right outside the flats. Catch all the passing trade, all the Olympic shit. *(SEAN pulls the flap back down and walks outside.)* Do you have any idea how many people are gonna be walking past there? There are going to be thousands of 'em, and once they get inside it'll be a rip-off. I was reading that everything's gonna be 86 percent more expensive in there than it is out here. They'll be crying out for something normal, something real, proper London.

RAY   How doyou get the punters to clock this thing?

SEAN presses play on a tape and Garage classic Double 99 by Rip Groove plays loudly out of speakers on top of the van. SEAN picks up a microphone and switches it on.

SEAN   *(Speaking through microphone.)* Drinks, burgers, hotdogs, souvenirs. Come and get it sports fans. Proper London food, served by proper London boys, to some proper London tunes! *(The beat drops as he says "tunes". RAY and SEAN both have a second or two of bobbing slightly to the beat.)* So, you in?

RAY   No, thanks for the offer but…

SEAN   Don't you like money?

RAY   I do but…iss my birthday coming up.

SEAN   Oh yeah?

RAY   Yeah and I've got tickets to the 10 metre air pistol shooting and…

SEAN   Ten metre air pistol shooting!

RAY   I know. Iss gonna be sick!

SEAN   Geez, this is a big opportunity. It ain't gonna come round again.

RAY   Yeah but I've got a bit of money from the Nazis and I've got bit of other business that I'm doing, if you know what I mean, and I'd quite like to enjoy my birthday and the bloody

Olympic Games arriving on my doorstep. Anyway, I thought we was supposed to be practising for that set in Leyton next week. The whole crew's coming down: Mike, Perry... And that booking agent who does all the clubs in the south of England is maybe gonna be there. We're still going to play, right?

SEAN   Course.

RAY   I'm telling you, it's gonna be massive. We don't want to take our eyes off the prize.

SEAN   We can do both. Come on, geez.

RAY   Why the sudden rush to become Sir Alan's next apprentice anyway?

SEAN   Look, I just really need your help, alright?

Pause.

RAY   Oh, you stupid...not again. Who do you owe this time? Not Cod's Eyes. Tell me you don't owe Cod's Eyes. Oh, you bloody mug. What is it with you? You see a pack of anorexic dogs chasing Sooty round a bleeding track and your wallet comes out like that.

SEAN   Just meet me here tomorrow, will ya?

RAY   Course mate. What time?

SEAN   Four.

RAY   Alright. I'll see you later then.

SEAN   Where you going now?

RAY   Carpenters. I'm meeting the crew for the closing down party. We're all going dressed as students, you know, bit of a joke about the new university campus. There's gonna be a lock-in later. Can you believe it? The amount of bloody times I've asked Seamus for a lock-in and it's finally happening.

SEAN   Except when we do leave he's gonna lock us out for good.

RAY   Yeah, it's a crying shame. But don't you worry – onwards and upwards. I was telling Mike and Perry last night, if it comes to it the crew can always meet at the our tree in the park, you know, just like back in the day – branch each, radio locked to Freek FM 101.8, beer, zoot – happy days. *(Beat.)* Oi, now don't you go worrying about Cod's Eyes. We're gonna sort this mess out, alright? OK, see ya later.

SEAN   Later. *(RAY exits, as soon as he is gone, SEAN picks up the phone and dials.)* Chelle, iss me. *(Pause.)* Yeah, don't start, alright – look, I've gone into business. *(Pause.)* Yeah, I bought a burger van. *(Pause.)* Serious. I'm parking it outside the flats. We're gonna get that two grand for the deposit. If you wanna live in Chobham Manor, we'll live in Chobham Manor. Forget the set in Leyton. I'm not doing it. *(Beat.)* And, guess what? I read some of that book you left behind and it said I'm experiencing the nesting instinct. It said people get it at different times, so I guess in my case it just come on late, but now it has and it feels good, really good. Yeah, serious. I'm like a pigeon or something *(Pause.)* no, a nice pigeon a beautiful...more like a dove *(Pause.)* OK, not a pigeon, some other bird, what are those big ones, no, you know, an emu or something, I'm an emu and what I'm saying is I'm really trying to build us a nest and when it's ready we're all gonna fly there *(Pause.)* no, we'll take my mum's car but you see what I'm saying? We're both emus and soon we're going to fly off to the nest which I'm building so that you can lay the egg and we can be a happy family of emus. *(Pause.)* It was, yeah. Rod Hull. *(Pause.)* No they don't all attack people. *(Pause.) (Shouting.)* OK, not a fucking emu then! *(Pause.)* I'm not shouting, babe. I'm not. I'm sorry. *(Pause.)* Iss just me, on my own. No one else involved. Don't hang up, babe. Truss me, Chelle, you'll see, I'll do us proud. *(CHELLE hangs up.)* Chelle...

Blackout.

JEREMY HUNT, SECRETARY OF STATE FOR CULTURE, OLYMPICS, MEDIA AND SPORT (V.O.)

I think we've always been very very proud of our country and proud of our culture and this is a chance to show off the best of Britain to the world.

Second of radio tuning or static noise then cut to:

JEREMY HUNT, SECRETARY OF STATE FOR CULTURE, OLYMPICS,
    MEDIA AND SPORT (V.O.)
    Amazing tourism attractions, the strength of our national
    brand. This is a very very unique moment to bang the
    national drum.

SCENE 3

*Outside the flats. The van is set up with the lights on and the flap up. We now see
SEAN and RAY at work, serving their wares to an unseen queue of people. The idea
is to get a sense of them beavering away. The lighting suggests speeded-up time.
This little section takes place over an optimistic UK Garage tune. The music cuts
out after a minute or two and we return immediately to the action.*

SEAN   We was properly on it, mate!

RAY   Dyou see how long that queue was? I swear it went all the way
           to them bollards. How much we made?

SEAN   Iss in the drawer, geez. We're juss getting started. Thass one
           afternoon in that drawer. Imagine how much'll be in there
           after two weeks of this! Remember we gotta stay with it. We're
           gonna get 'em all again on the way out.

RAY   Yes chef.

RAY opens the door.

SEAN   Where you going?

RAY   For a snout, chef. You coming? Might not have time later.

SEAN   OK, better put the flap down.

RAY   Yes chef.

SEAN   Stop calling me that.

RAY   Sorry Chef.

RAY goes to the flap and pulls it down.

SEAN   Easy does it.

RAY and SEAN both walk out of the van and light cigarettes.

RAY   I can't believe you didn't make it down last night. Whole crew
             was there. Mike, Perry… I went as Jeremy Clarkson from
             University Challenge.

SEAN   Thass Jeremy Paxman.

RAY   Yeah, thass what I said, Jeremy Pacman. Seamus was handing
             out the drinks like never before.

SEAN   How was he?

RAY   He was fine until right at the end and then he got, you know, a
             bit emotional. 22 years he's run that place.

SEAN   What's he gonna do now?

RAY   Said he's not sure. Said he knew deep down it was all over
             a year ago when he got everything ready for the pub quiz
             one night: sign up, printed out all the questions, sharpened a
             load of pencils and when it got to 8 in the evening there was
             no one there, no one, just him on his jones. Said he read the
             questions out loud through the mic because he didn't want his
             Mrs upstairs to hear that it was another flop.

SEAN   Why didn't he get out then?

RAY   Dunno. Guess he wasn't ready to call time on it. Probably
             convinced himself it was still a success, you know, just to
             keep going but then the new university campus, well, the
             students won't wanna go to the Carpenters, will they? *(KEITH,
             a Glaswegian man of about the same age as RAY and SEAN, walks up
             to them.)* Keith mate. How you been?

KEITH   Alright, yeah, yeah. Bit mental innit, but, aye, no bad.

RAY   You know Sean, don't ya?
KEITH   Course, yeah. So, wass all this? Wass happened to DJ Slinky
             and MC Sting-Ray?

RAY   This is temporary, geez. We've got a couple of bookings
             coming up.

KEITH   Oh, well, let me know, yeah? I love all that stuff. *(Badly
             beatboxes a garage beat, as if to prove he is a fan and sways to his
             own beat).* I remember that night you played at that place next
             to the Rex. That was you, werntit? Fuckin' fantastic.

SEAN   July 2002?

KEITH   Aye, that'd be about right. Good memory, this wan's got, eh? *(Pause.)* What? What did I…? Oh, thass right, intit? There was that fuck-up. You was supposed to play at some massive club on the party island, werntyous?

RAY   Yeah, thanks for reminding me, Keith.

KEITH   Ayia bloody Napa. That woulda been quite a gig, eh? Imagine all the lasses out there. Dancing away in their bikinis, desperate for sex, especially with a big M.C. like you, Ray.

RAY   Cheers Keith.

KEITH   You gotti look on the bright side though, Ray. You might think you missed out but that much sex isnae good fer a man – different girl every night, ravenous sexual appetites, that'd take sommat outta yer. Every cloud, thass what I'm saying. If you hadnae got arrested fer nabbing that Ronald McDonald statue, you and Sean wouldae caught that plane to Ayia Napa and, yes, you'd now be a famous garage MC and, yes, youda had more sex, a heck of a lot more but at what cost, Ray? Ronald McDonald may well have saved your soul.

RAY   It wasn't Ronald McDonald.

KEITH   Was it not?

RAY   It was the Little Chef.

KEITH   Hahahahaha. Of course the fucking Little Chef. I'd call it the Wee Chef, but it doesnae have the right ring to it down here, does it? *(Beat.)* Why dyou nick the Wee Chef?

RAY   Why do we do anything, Keith?

   Pause.

SEAN   What can I do for you, Keith? Hotdog, burger…?

KEITH   Actually I was… Ray said he might be able to sort me out with a wee bit of something. Bit a Mandy.

RAY   No problemo.

   RAY produces a bag.

SEAN   Shit mate, where doyou get all that?

RAY   *(To KEITH.)* Walk this way, mate. *(RAY walks to the side of the van, followed by KEITH.)* How much dyou want?

KEITH   Two wraps?

RAY   Thass a gram each. So that's 60.

KEITH   60!

RAY   This is the shit, mate. Truss me. Do a line of it now if you
              don't believe me.

KEITH   Aye, OK.

*RAY carefully pushes up the flap of the van and chops up two lines on the serving
counter.*

RAY   *(Calling to SEAN.)* You want one, geez.

SEAN   No mate, we need to stay on it.

RAY   There's nothing happening. Everyone's at the ceremony. We
              got hours. I'm aving one. Here you go, Keith. Tell me that's
              not the bollocks.

KEITH does a line of MDMA off the counter.

KEITH   Fuck me, that hurts.

RAY   No pain, no gain. Definitely don't want one, Sean?

SEAN   No.

RAY   How about a pipe and slippers then, granddad? Hahaha. Oi,
              Keith, you remember when Sean was a laugh?

KEITH   Aye. Hanging out with Sean's shite. I'd rather watch a box set
              of fuckin *Downton Abbey.*

SEAN   Shut up!

KEITH   Mebbe he's goingto watch *Downton Abbey* after this. Thass
              what you're into isn't it, Sean? *(Doing Downton Abbey but with
              his Glaswegian accent.)* Lady Fucknose, I do consider you a
              most unsuitable match for Lord Cuntyballs.

RAY   Are you gonna take that, Sean? Are you gonna take that?
              There's a line right here for ya.

SEAN   Oh, sod it, go on then.

*As SEAN lifts his head from snorting a line of MDMA powder, we hear the
famous chorus of "Land of Hope and Glory" coming from the Opening Ceremony.*

Blackout.

BRITISH PRIME MINISTER DAVID CAMERON (V.O)
> As we welcome the world to the best Olympics ever, and as, in the 60th year of her reign, we honour our queen as the finest and most famous example of British dedication, British duty, British steadiness, British tradition, let us use these things as a mirror of ourselves too, a mirror of the nation – resilient, realitic, curious, enterprising, intelligent, inventive, unswerving.

SCENE 4

The van is blasting out UK Garage pretty loudly. SEAN and RAY have abandoned the vehicle and are standing around with drinks and cigarettes gently dancing to the music. KEITH is still there too and now they have been joined by a strikingly beautiful and exotic woman who is dancing in her own little world.

KEITH   I'm fucked!

SEAN   Alright, Keith, steady on.

KEITH   I'm going for another one. You coming?

SEAN   I'm alright, geez.

KEITH   Ray?

SEAN   Ray don't need another one. I can't have him giving away any more burgers.

RAY   Amount we sold, we can afford to give a few away. Business is all about brand loyalty. *(KEITH goes to van.)* Don't get much better than this, geez. Rinsing choons outside the block with your best mate.

SEAN   No. No, it don't. *(Beat.)* Ray, there's…
RAY   It feels…it feels kinda…it really feels like…there's something about being here, you know, being here, outside the block – I'm from here, you're from here… It really feels… *(Tails off.)*

SEAN   Ray, there's something…

RAY   It really feels…it just really feels… I dunno…

SEAN   Ray, there's…

RAY   It really feels…it feels like…

SEAN   Jesus, Ray! Are you trying to say it feels nice to be at home?

RAY   Yep, thass the one. Don't you agree?

SEAN   Course I bloody agree. *(Beat.)* Oi, you seen her?

RAY   Yeah.

SEAN   She has got some moves. Wheredshe come from? *(RAY gives the same look as before.)* No!

RAY   Groundbait, geez – pulls 'em in from far and wide. What did I say? Ducks in a barrel.

SEAN   Well, what are you waiting for? Phase Two, yeah?

RAY   You don't rush Phase Two, Sean. You approach the water with great caution, you make sure your lure is tied securely to the line and only then do you cast.

SEAN   Well I think this one might swim off if you don't hurry. Go and bloody talk to her.

RAY   What, now?

SEAN   Well, I'm not going to am I and Keith's long gone. I don't think he's said anything for an hour.

RAY   OK. Phase Two. Watch and learn. *(RAY sort of dances over to where CARMELA is dancing. Her impressive moves contrast with RAY's ineptitude. RAY struggles to make his approach because she is constantly moving. When he does get close she still doesn't notice him. She only realises he is there when he opens his mouth and speaks far too loudly right in her face. CARMELA jumps.)* Isn't the Olympics brilliant!

CARMELA What? I'm sorry, my English…

RAY   I love the way it inspires a whole new generation to…

CARMELA I'm sorry, my English. I don't…

RAY   Where are you from?

CARMELA Panama. *(Pause.)*
             Central America.

RAY   Oh. Do you like football?

CARMELA No.

RAY   Me neither.

CARMELA But you are wearing a football shirt.

Pause.

RAY   OK, see you later.

Admitting defeat, RAY sort of half dances, half shuffles away back to where SEAN is standing.

SEAN   How dyou get on?

RAY   Well as could be expected.

SEAN   Yeah?

RAY   She's from Panama. Do you know anything about Panama?

SEAN   Why?

RAY   I just need a way in.

SEAN   Well, there's the canal.

RAY   I can't ask her about the canal.

SEAN   Why not?

RAY   Too obvious.

SEAN   Don't talk about Panama then, just ask her something else, why you got to talk to her about Panama?

RAY   Yeah, you're right. I'll just open up another conversation – nothing to do with Panama.

SEAN   OK. Back you go, son. Reel her in.

RAY dances back towards CARMELA.

RAY   My name's Ray.

CARMELA Carmela.

Pause.

RAY   Have you ever been to the old Panama canal?

CARMELA Yes.

RAY   Is it…big?

CARMELA Gigantic.

RAY   While you're here you should check out the River Lea. There are some nice benches and you can sit there and, you know, watch the ducks.

CARMELA Is it big?

RAY   Piece of string really.

CARMELA What?

RAY   How long's a piece of string? No way of knowing.

CARMELA Well, the Panama canal is 82km long.

RAY   Don't work like that over here. *(Pause.)* What about the hats then?

CARMELA What about them?

RAY   Does everyone wear 'em?

CARMELA They come from Ecuador.

RAY   OK, see you later.

RAY shuffles back to the safety of SEAN.

SEAN   Any good?

RAY   Think I'm just gonna play it cool for a bit.

SEAN   She's into the music, geez. Why don't you get on the mic?

RAY   Nah, I'm licked mate. Might be best to let this one go.

SEAN   Come on, thass never stopped you before and look at her for Christ's sake!

RAY   I am looking at her.

SEAN   Come on, what about those new lyrics, be good practice for Friday.

RAY   OK, you choose something.

SEAN goes into the van and puts on an instrumental UK Garage track. He emerges a moment later with the microphone and speaks into it to introduce RAY.

SEAN   Now, ladies and gentlemen iss time for something a little bit special. Make some noise for the one and only, the Stratford Pavarotti, Emmmmmmmmmm, seeeeeeeeeeee, Sting-Ray!

SEAN passes the microphone to RAY. CARMELA moves closer to where RAY is standing, followed by KEITH who seems only dimly aware of his surroundings.

RAY   *(Initially nervously.)* Testing testing, one, one, two, mic check. One, two, testing. Mic check. Going out to the one-like Keith, the one like DJ Slinky.

Stingray on the M.I.C, I dive on the mic like Tom Daley,
Don't tess, Don't meddle,
I take gold like a garage Beth Tweddle.
Watch and learn my lyrics keep flowing
Me on the mic is like Redgrave rowing.
Not Vanessa, I mean Steven
Don't need Pinsent to keep my stroke even
Back in the day, when I was a pup,
Seen Akabusi smack it up.
Seen the legends come and go,
Steve Backley's 90-metre throw,
Searle Brothers and the crying cox,
Gold medal for Linford's lunchbox,
Is it a con? Is it a ploy?
Billions of pounds just to watch Chris Hoy,
Go round and round on a stupid bike,
Stratford's changing for sports we don't like.
So now the Olympics has come to my home,
The flats are overlooked by a velodrome. You have to wonder wass it all for?
Do they think we're all fans of Anish Kapoor?
It's tough to say what these games will bring
Can't be worth it to hear Macca sing,
'Hey Jude, don't take it bad'
Who the fuck is Jude?
He can't still be sad
Shut up Paul you're not my real dad

Now this honey's outside the flat,

I'd tried it on like a Panama hat
If she likes my lyrics, she'll give
me a kiss
If she don't I hope she won't see this
As the time she got chirpsed by a fat man
Who swore to her blind he's not West Ham.

SEAN   Yes mate, that was sick.

KEITH   Nice one, bruv, seriously. That was…

CARMELA That was fantastic.

SEAN   Did you hear him namecheck you and all?

CARMELA Yes. That was…

SEAN   So does he get a kiss or what?

CARMELA strides confidently up to RAY and gives him a long kiss on the lips.

KEITH   *(Rapping very badly.)* My name's Keith McGregor and I come from Scot-land, when I was a wee lad, I used to play in a marching band, I practiced the triangle every day, Til my big brother Craig said I looked…

SEAN pushes KEITH away from RAY and CARMELA.

SEAN   *(To KEITH.)* What you doing?

RAY and CARMELA stop kissing.

KEITH   Oi Ray, less go for another one, eh? *(Beat.)* Come on!

RAY   Yeah, OK. *(To CARMELA.)* You in? *(CARMELA shrugs.)* You coming for one, Sean?

SEAN   Nah.

RAY   Oh, come on, geez.

SEAN   OK, juss one more though. *(They all start to walk towards the van.)* Stand guard for a sec willya, Keith?

SEAN puts the flap down on the van as RAY and CARMELA enter.

Immediately CHELLE appears carrying a large sports hold-all. She approaches KEITH who is very far gone.

CHELLE   Dyou know my boyfriend?

KEITH   Who's your boyfriend?
CHELLE   Sean. This is his van.

KEITH   No. Not ringing any bells.

Long pause.

CHELLE   You sure you don't know where my…
KEITH   *(Interrupting.)* My girlfriend left me last week. Said I wasnae assertive enough.

CHELLE   Why you telling me this?

KEITH   Juss making a bita conversation, you know. It's OK though –
             thanks fer asking – I'm going tae a seminar tomorrow morning
             at 10. It's called "Awaken the Giant Within." Mebbes then
             she'll come back.

CHELLE   Right, OK mate.

KEITH   Watch this space: new beginning. 10 a.m. tomorrow. Giant
             awakes.

CHELLE   OK, well, good luck with that.

*Suddenly much amplified out of the top of the van comes the sound of SEAN
snorting a line of MDMA.*

SEAN   Fuck that hurts. Shit. Oh fuck that's strong. Woooohooo. Get's
             you right in the back of the… What's that noise? Ray, the
             fucking mic.

Click. The mic is switched off.

KEITH   Sean's in the van.

CHELLE strides straight up to the van and starts hammering on the door.

SEAN   Chill out, Keith. You're up next.

CHELLE   Iss not Keith.

SEAN   Chelle, alright darling. *(SEAN opens the door.)*
             We're just doing a quick stock check before we close up.

CHELLE   Stock check.

SEAN   Yeah, how many burgers do we have?

RAY   Fuck knows. Shitloads.

CHELLE   Is that Ray?

SEAN   No.

RAY emerges.

RAY   Alright Lady Chelle. *(Pointing at her belly.)* How's the Little
             Hammer?
             (CARMELA appears at the door.)
             Do you know…?

CARMELA Carmela.

CHELLE   Oi, what the fuck is going on here, Sean?
             (RAY and CARMELA slip out of the van out of CHELLE's way.)

(Spitting mad.) I couldn't sleep at Natalie's. So I thought I'd come over and surprise you when you was closing up and… I thought you was supposed to be making some money, not… look at you. When you called me this morning I thought, oh he's finally doing something, finally trying to make things better for us for our family but iss the same old story, innit? You and Ray, the tunes, the drugs the…

SEAN   Well, we are just closing up, honest. I'll be up to bed in a tick if you did want to stay.

CHELLE   You think I'd go near you like this? You gotta be taking the piss.

CHELLE starts to walk off. SEAN follows her right to the edge of the stage, pleading with her until she is out of sight.

SEAN   Where you going?

CHELLE   Back to Natalie's. May as well get some more tips on being a single mum.

SEAN   Chelle, we've done well, we was just letting our hair down after a busy… Come on babe…

CHELLE   *(Crying.)* Just leave me alone will you, Sean? You're all talk, int ya, juss like your old man. Mean well, lots of good intentions but when it comes to it your heart's in the bookies or down the pub with your mates.

SEAN   Chelle, we…

CHELLE   I never thought that I'd end up like this, Sean. Look at me. One of those women who stands outside the flats crying, screaming her lungs out at her feller at one in the morning and everyone inside can hear it all and they think what a chav, what a piece of shit. I hate that you done this to me.

SEAN   Chelle, come on…

CHELLE   Don't touch me.

CHELLE starts to exit. SEAN follows her to the edge of the stage.

SEAN   Chelle, you got the wrong idea, babe. Don't juss walk off. How can we… *(SEAN is about to follow her off.)* Ray, you're in charge, watch the van, I got to… *(SEAN turns to see RAY kissing CARMELA.)* Oh, Jesus Christ!

CARMELA *(To RAY.)* Where do you live?

RAY   Here. 16th floor.

CARMELA Let's go there.

RAY   To mine?

CARMELA I come in for a cup of coffee?

RAY   *(With a note of panic.)* Coffee, you're sure you want…

The sound of police sirens.

SEAN   Oh Christ. Turn the music off. Turn the music off. Shit. We gotta go.

RAY   Chill geez, what, we can't play some music, celebrate the Olympics?

SEAN   No license. They'll take the van.

Blackout, followed by loud shouts from SEAN, RAY and KEITH. We then hear the noisy sound of the van starting up and backfiring several times before driving off.

JEREMY HUNT, SECRETARY OF STATE FOR CULTURE, OLYMPICS, MEDIA AND SPORT (V.O.)

Quiet British efficiency. Quiet British efficiency. And we all feel very very proud and it's fantastic.

Sound of radio tuning or static. Cut to:

DAVID CAMERON (V.O.)

It gives us an extraordinary incentive to look outwards, to look onwards, to feel pride in who we are and to look our best.

SCENE 5

The lights come up to find the van in a field. Birdsong. SEAN is lying on his back on the ground asleep in only a pair of Y-fronts. He gets up slowly. He is confused. He clearly has no idea where he is. He goes to the van and peers in at the door. He looks at his phone and then goes back to the door and peers in.

SEAN   Ray, wake up. Wake up, Ray. We've gotta get out of here. Get up, geez.

The van begins to sway with the movement of someone getting up. RAY swings open the door to the van and stands there also wearing only a pair of pants.

RAY   What a night! What a bloody night!

SEAN   Morning.

RAY   Jesus, where are we?

SEAN   I was hoping you'd know.

RAY   Last I remember is turning off the A112.

SEAN   I don't remember discussing a trip to the countryside. Do you?

RAY   No, geez. Maybe Keith knows.

SEAN   Keith? Did he come with us?

RAY   I don't know. I thought he did.

SEAN   No, we left him behind when we drove off. Where the bloody hell are we?
          We've gotta get back, geez. We should be opening for business again. What time is it?

RAY looks at phone.

RAY   Iss 11:45.

SEAN   I'll see if I can find out where we are.

RAY   Might wanna put some clothes on.

SEAN   Is she err…

RAY   Asleep, mate.

SEAN goes in and comes back a second later with his clothes which he puts on as he talks.

SEAN   Howdyou get on?

RAY   It was…it was pretty special.

SEAN   Nice one, geez. Nice one. *(Flashing the wad of cash.)*
          Well this is how well we got on. Not bad for a day's work.

RAY   Thass gotta be 500 right there and thass just the notes.

SEAN   Count it for us willya? I'll be back in two ticks.
          SEAN wanders off. RAY sits down on a log and begins to count the money. CARMELA appears at the door wearing RAY's West Ham shirt like a nightie. She sees RAY and walks over. She puts her arm around RAY.

RAY   Morning. How's the head?

CARMELA I feel like, how do you say, in my country we say, in the head
          we have this animal, like the little animals, cangrejo, you
          know, they look like this… *(She mimes what looks like some kind
          of insect.)*

RAY   Flies.

CARMELA No, like this, you know.

RAY   Prawns.

CARMELA *(Doing pincers.)* No, like this, at the beach.

RAY   Crabs?

CARMELA Yes! I have crabs!
          (RAY bursts out laughing.) Why you laugh at me, baby?

RAY   Forget it. Come and sit over here with me.

CARMELA Where is your Slinky friend?

RAY   Went to find out where we are.
          (Holding up the cash.) I'm the numbers guy. We gotta get back
          soon. I don't see what the rush is meself. We could just chill
          here for a bit, couldn't we, me and you. We could go for a
          walk if you like and if we find a shop, maybe we could get
          something to eat, something to drink, have a bit of a picnic.
          Lazy Saturday in the countryside.

CARMELA Oh my god. Madre mia, por dios, oi, que voy hacer. No lo
          creo. No lo creo.

RAY   What! What are you saying?

CARMELA Saturday! I have to leave. I am physiotherapist for the
          Olympic team, we have lunch today with the President.

RAY   Yeah, I had the 10m air pistol shooting at 11. You'll have to
          sack it off.

CARMELA I have to leave right now. Oh, how will I get back all the way
          to London? Please give me some of the money. I must find a
          taxi.
          *(CARMELA whips the football shirt off and starts getting changed
          into the clothes she was wearing the night before. RAY is entranced.)*
          Please give me as much as you can. I will pay you back, all of
          it, I promise.

RAY   Well…

CARMELA How much is there?

RAY   That's about 500 altogether…

CARMELA Give me 400, please.

RAY   Well, thass a lot…

CARMELA I just need to leave right now… *(She grabs the money kisses him and takes a large wad of it.)* I don't know how much it will cost but I will get it all back to you tomorrow, I promise.

RAY   OK, how will you find me?

CARMELA You gave me your number last night.

> *CARMELA kisses him again.*

> Tomorrow. I will see you tomorrow. Which way should I go?

RAY   Sounds like there's a road that way but look, we'll probably be off in a bit and…

> *CARMELA walks off in the opposite direction to SEAN. RAY goes inside and gets his trousers and stuffs the remaining money into his jeans. SEAN enters.*

SEAN   Well, no bloody clue where we are. Get your bird up, we've gotta get moving.

RAY   She's gone. Listen, she really couldn't hang about so, don't get angry but I've given her some of the money to get a cab.

SEAN   How much?

RAY   About 400.

SEAN   Oh, you stupid, you stupid.
                 Tell me you fucked her.

RAY   What?

SEAN   At least tell me you fucked her, Ray.

RAY   Don't worry, geez, we're just getting to know each other.

SEAN   So it cost 600 quid not to screw her.

RAY   No, I told you, I've only give her 400 and she'll pay me back.

SEAN   And what about the 200 me, Mike and Perry give her?

RAY   What?

SEAN   That's right. Happy Birthday, Ray! Happy 30th!

RAY   Was you gonna tell me?

Pause.

SEAN   Come on, Ray. You thought a bird like that is gonna go for
                 you?

Pause.

RAY   *(Almost breaking.)* I just thought my luck was in, Sean, if you
                 must know. Yep, I thought finally my luck was in.

RAY begins to walk in the direction of the van.

SEAN   It was Mike and Perry's idea. We just didn't want you to hit 30
                 without…you know.

RAY   You can all get fucked. I'm pleased I give her the 400. *(RAY gets
                 into van. Suddenly he flings open the flap at the front and shouts.)*
                 Don't think I'm gonna help you earn the money back neither.
                 I'm out!

*Almost instantly the four walls of the van begin to sway. Now they fall outwards
one after another and come crashing to the ground leaving only the frame of the
chassis. Crammed right to the front of the van, KEITH is revealed asleep under
a tarpaulin. He sits up startled.*

KEITH   What time is it? *(Looks at watch.)* Shit.

SEAN runs over to the van and stands for a moment surveying the wreckage.

SEAN   What have you done? You fucking…

RAY   I told you this was a heap of shit. It ain't my fault, if you go
                 and buy some clapped out…

SEAN   Don't you fucking start, I told you you gotta be careful you fat
                 fuck and then you go slamming that open you fucking retard.
                 *(KEITH covers himself back up with the tarpaulin. RAY's phone beeps.
                 He looks at it.)* Don't look at your fucking phone, start thinking
                 about how we're gonna…

RAY   *(Interrupting.)* Iss from Perry. He says he tried to call you ten
                 times already but you never picked up.

SEAN   Why?

RAY   Your baby's on the way.

Blackout.

JEREMY HUNT, SECRETARY OF STATE FOR CULTURE, OLYMPICS, MEDIA AND SPORT (V.O.)

It's a chance for us Brits to show everyone that when it comes to efficient organisation we can do it better, than anyone else in the world.

SCENE 6

A hospital waiting room. CHELLE and her younger sister NATALIE are sitting, waiting to be seen. A reception desk is unmanned. NATALIE is white but she speaks with a strong London rude-girl accent.

CHELLE   What the hell is the delay here?

NATALIE   Iss a joke, I swear. When that butters receptionist gets back I'm gonna be up in her fayce, you know. I'll be like: you said 20 minutes, we been here over an ow-ar, yeah? You can't leave my sis-tar out here in lay-bar like dat. I don't care. I'll be like, question: do you fink that is an appropriate way to treat my sis-tar when she's in lay-bar?

SEAN burst into the room. He is out of breath.

SEAN   Chelle, Nat, thank god. I thought you mighta already gone through.

CHELLE   What you doing here?

SEAN   Perry rang. He said he seen you getting into a cab. I got here as soon as I could.

NATALIE   Yeah, but, hang on – question:…

SEAN   *(Interrupting.)* Nat, I know what you're…

NATALIE   *(Interrupting.)* Have you heard me arks a question, Sean?

SEAN   OK, wass your bloody question?

NATALIE   Is you the birfing part-nar?

SEAN   Yeah but…

NATALIE   Not yeah, Sean, not yeah, nooo. You ain't the birfing part-nar.

SEAN   OK, yeah, I know, Natalie, I know but…

CHELLE　*(Contraction.)* Ohh fuccck…

SEAN　Look, I'm here now and I want to…why are we still waiting anyway?

NATALIE　Bitch receptionist, innit? *(Kisses teeth.)*

SEAN　Has no one seen you?

CHELLE　No!

SEAN　Don't worry, Chelle, I'll sort this out.

SEAN walks over to a door leading to the examination area. He knocks loudly.

NATALIE　Do you fink I didn't try dat already? Dickhead! *(Kisses teeth.)*

SEAN　*(Calling through door.)* Hello. Is there anyone in there? When are we gonna get seen?

Enter RAY with a plastic bag.

RAY　Alright, Lady Chelle, alright Natalie.

NATALIE　Oh my dayz, who invited the Fat Controw-lar? Hahahaha.

CHELLE　Wass he doing here?

RAY　I dropped Sean off in my car. There was…

SEAN　There was a problem with the van. What do you want, Ray?

RAY　I thought I'd bring something for Chelle. Here.

RAY hands plastic bag to NATALIE.

NATALIE　Oi, what the hell is diss?

RAY　Red Bull and a Ginsters – always sorts me out.

NATALIE　Do you think she's coming back from a rayve or summing? Wass she gonna do with this?

RAY　I could see if there's a microwave.

Door opens. A male MIDWIFE enters.

MIDWIFE　Michelle Baines.

CHELLE　Finally!

MIDWIFE　We're just going to take you through into the examination area to see how things are progressing and with any luck we should be able to admit you to the delivery suite very shortly.

NATALIE　Bout time. *(Beat.)* Is you a midwife?

MIDWIFE　Yes.

NATALIE   Ahahaha. Jokes!

SEAN goes over to CHELLE and starts to help her to her feet to walk through into the examination area.

MIDWIFE   Sir, I'm afraid hospital policy is that there are no male partners in the examination area. You're perfectly entitled of course to come through into the delivery suite when the time comes.

NATALIE   Yeah but, midwife, he ain't the birthing part…

SEAN   *(Interrupting.)* Can't we both go through into…

MIDWIFE   *(Interrupting.)* Only one person can go in with mum, I'm afraid. *(Looks down at notes for name.)* Michelle, you'll have to decide. OK, this way, we won't be long.

NATALIE   Go back to your stupid van, Sean, rinse your choons wiv Ray. I'll call you when the baby's here, if I got enough minutes.

NATALIE takes CHELLE's arm and they follow the MIDWIFE off into the examination area, leaving SEAN and RAY alone.

SEAN   Don't open your mouth, OK?

RAY   Is that your way of saying thank you for driving you here after what you done to me with Carmela?

SEAN   Am I supposed to thank you for destroying my van? For getting me stuck in the middle of Epping Forest?

RAY   Where doyou buy that van? Toys R Us?

SEAN   Look, juss go home, willya? Just fuck off and leave me to it.

RAY   OK, Sean, I will fuck off. You know, I didn't even want to help you. The only reason I done it is because you can't walk past a Ladbrokes without your dick going hard. Great father you're gonna be: "Child Benefit, yeah, lovely, stick it all on the 12:05 at Milton Keynes."

SEAN   You don't know what you're talking about. I packed in the gambling.

RAY   Oh yeah, course you have – tell that to Cod's Eyes.

SEAN   I don't owe Cod's Eyes.

RAY   Oh, brilliant, so who do you owe?

SEAN   I don't owe no one.

RAY   Let me guess: there's some other mug down the bookies and
           he owes you, so when he gives you the money, you'll be able
           to…

SEAN   You're not listening to me: I don't owe no one.

RAY   So, why the fuckin hell have we spent the last 48 hours doing
           business from that Ikea flatpack?

SEAN   I'm getting out.

RAY   What?

SEAN   We're leaving the block, Ray. We're moving to the new flats.

RAY   What? You can't.

Enter MIDWIFE with NATALIE and CHELLE in a wheelchair.

MIDWIFE   So, I'll just leave you here for two minutes while I go and see
           if the delivery suite is ready.

NATALIE   Fanks, mid-WIFE. Ahahaha. *(Beat.)* You should be a mid-
           husband, innit? You should talk to your boss…I'd be like,
           question: do you fink a man can be a wiyfe? *(MIDWIFE looks at
           her utterly bemused.)* De ans-arr to diss question is noooo.

MIDWIFE exits.

SEAN   Chelle, I want to be the one who comes through with you. I
           know I haven't been taking enough interest in the baby but
           I've changed…

NATALIE   *(Stroking her chin.)* Oh my dayz, dere's a beard growing right
           on my chin. Look at my beard. Captain Birdseye inda house!

SEAN   Natalie! Please! Chelle, I've been…I've been trying hard these
           last few days, I started a business and I've been earning good
           money, proper money.

CHELLE   So, have you got the money?

Pause.

SEAN   There was…there was an issue. We had some of the money!
           We made a lot in one day but…

NATALIE   Dere's always a but intthere? Wass the but, Sean?

CHELLE   Let me guess, Mr Blobby over here lost the lot. Same old
           story, eh?

NATALIE   Mr Blobby. Ahahah.

SEAN   You know what he's like…

CHELLE   I don't believe it. I tellya not to involve him. I tellya to… everything I'm saying is trying to get you away from him… and you go and wass wrong with you, Sean? Iss like bloody Ayia Napa all over again!

    Beat.

NATALIE Dese boys are jowkars, Chelle. What did I tellya? Thass why I'm the birfing part-nar. And thass why when we leave here you're coming to my gaff wiv your yout.

SEAN   Chelle, listen to me: I want to be there for you and our little boy.

NATALIE So, where's he been for the last 9 months, Chelle?

SEAN   We go in there the two of us, yeah, and I support you through it and we come out together, a family.

NATALIE How's he gonna support a family?

CHELLE   I don't need this now, Sean.

SEAN   I wanna be the one who carries him through the door into our home.

CHELLE   I can't be dealing with this now.

SEAN   I know, so when that midwife comes back in here just tell him that you want the boy's father to come through with you.

NATALIE Oi, don't try to trick her like dat. Where was you, Sean, when she went into lay-bar? Where was you when…

    Unseen by the others, RAY has walked calmly to the back of the room and has stood on a chair.

SEAN   Don't listen to her, Chelle. You're making a mistake. You've made your point and now I'm here and I'm begging you to let me be here for this.

NATALIE Chelle, don't take him back. He don't have no interest in this yout. I'm telling you. You think he'll help you out? You think he'll change any nappies? Man ain't a bloke, he's a joke, he'll get straight on the phone line to his bredren Ray, talking about his choons and…

RAY   *(Shouting above everyone else.)* Oi!

    Silence.

SEAN Ray, what you doing?

NATALIE Must be a toffee stuck to the ceiling, innit? Ahahahah.

RAY *(Sharply.)* Shut the fuck up, Natalie! *(Beat.)* I'm sorry, Chelle, but this ain't nothing like Ayia Napa.

CHELLE What?

SEAN Ray...

RAY *(Interrupting.)* I was ready to get on that plane.

CHELLE Eh?

RAY Thass right – bags packed, brand-new passport, ready to go but where was Sean? Not outside the flats like we agreed. Looked everywhere until eventually I went to our tree in West Ham park and there he was sitting under it, hood up, crying his eyes out.

SEAN Ray, please!

RAY I tried to drag him to the flats to pack his things but he wouldn't budge, sobbing he was. There was still time for me to go, to get to Stansted.

SEAN Not now, Ray.

RAY I coulda performed, Chelle, I coulda gone to those meetings, probably got signed but Sean begged me to stay: "Chelle'll dump me if she knows I bottled it. Let's say you done something stupid, Ray, everyone will believe that, so fat, stupid Ray says he nicked the Little Chef. That was the moment for me to become something better than what I am and he took it from me but I stuck by him and I bit my tongue and now he says you're leaving, going to make a better life. *(RAY gets down from chair and walks over to SEAN and CHELLE.)* But he can't leave, not after what I done for him.

CHELLE Sean, is this...?

SEAN Iss true. But I can leave, Ray. I have to. I'm sorry.

RAY exits. A pause.

NATALIE Question:...

CHELLE *(Interrupting.)* Nat! Why didn't you say nothing, Sean?

NATALIE Your man is a pussyhole, juss like his pops! You're better off without him. He don't know. *(Kisses teeth.)*

CHELLE Sean? Why didn't you tell me? Why did you blame Ray all this time?

Enter MIDWIFE. Pause.

SEAN I just...I was scared you wouldn't wanna be with that...with this. Better for you to think I was still in with a chance of makin it, you know, bita hope coz without that, what have we got? I thought you'd leave me, Chelle, and I couldn't let that happen, I can't let that happen. Thass why I'm standing here now begging you to take me back.

MIDWIFE Err. Hi. Sorry but, mum, the delivery suite is ready, so who'll be coming through with you?

Blackout.

SCENE 7

SEAN stands in a spotlight behind some decks on a podium in a club. A strobe effect. He is playing a UK Garage hit. The intense focus of a man at the top of his game, playing to thousands of people.

SEAN Loving your vibes down here Leyton. You lot are large. Right this one's going out to my bredren Norris da boss Windross, played here a few weeks back. Proper legend. I say Norris, you say da Boss, Norris:...I can't hear you! I say Norris, you say da Boss, Norris:...

The lighting shifts revealing the same room SEAN was standing in at the beginning of the play.

RAY They're leaving me.

SEAN *(Startled.)* Jesus. Howdyou get in?

RAY Door was on the latch.

SEAN Who's leaving you? What you talking about?

RAY The Nazis.

SEAN So what?

RAY	Iss sad to see em go. Nice couple. We got talking on our way to the hospital.
SEAN	Hospital? *(RAY holds up heavily bandaged hand.)* Booby traps?
RAY	Yep. Anyway they ended up driving me to the Homerton and we got chatting and turns out they're not Nazis, they're Buddhists.
SEAN	What about the…
RAY	Buddhist fertility symbol is exactly the same as the swastika apparently.
SEAN	You'd think that would cause problems in Germany.
RAY	Yeah but turns out they're from Latvia. Anyway, thass them gone.
SEAN	Long with everyone else.
RAY	See ya later.
SEAN	Much later.
RAY	Like never again. Ha!

Enter CHELLE bursting with energy.

CHELLE	Hello Ray.
RAY	Alright Lady Chelle.
SEAN	Alright babe.
	Wass up with you? Where's Archie?
CHELLE	Natalie's got him for a minute. I wanted to show you something.

Handing SEAN an envelope.

SEAN	Wass this? Newham council? What do they want?
CHELLE	Sean, I put the money down for the flat months ago.
SEAN	What? Whose money?
CHELLE	My mum's. Iss just a loan and we'll have to find a way to pay it all back.
SEAN	What?
CHELLE	Don't be angry. I couldn't wait for you to find the money, could I?

SEAN If it weren't for the van though Chelle, I'd have the…

CHELLE Less forget about it, Sean. It don't matter how – we got the money and this is our new start right here in this letter. *(Beat.)* Less open it now. I've had it all day and I waited to get home to open it with you.
(SEAN and RAY gather around.) I can't do it. Sean, you open it. Please say we got a balcony. Please say we got a balcony. And a view of the park. Balcony and a view of the park. Balcony and a view of the park.

SEAN opens the letter. He holds up a cheque.

SEAN Iss a cheque. *(Pause.)* "Due to the diminished allocation of shared purchase housing in Chobham Manor, we regret to inform you that you have not been selected for a property in this new development. We have added you to our mailing list and will be keeping you abreast of other shared purchase opportunities. Please find enclosed your cheque for two thousand pounds."

Long pause. Enter NATALIE with baby in pram.

NATALIE Fink he needs feeding, Chelle. What you lot standin round here for? Quick get the telly on. Iss the closing ceremony. Some geezer called Tom Jones is sposed to be doin a duet with that bitch Leo-nar Lewis. *(Kisses teeth.)*

She picks up the remote control and switches on the television. CHELLE goes to the pram and picks up the baby. They all gather in front of the television. SEAN puts his arm around CHELLE. A very slow fade as we hear the sound of Leona Lewis singing which melts away into the popping of fireworks, snatches of speeches. Once the lights are out, we hear the following audio from 2005:

JACQUES ROGGE, IOC PRESIDENT (V.O.)

    The International Olympic Committee has the honour of announcing that the games of the 30th Olympiad in 2012 are awarded to the city of London.

A few seconds of the ecstatic cheering which followed the announcement.

End.

WWW.OBERONBOOKS.COM

Follow us on www.twitter.com/@oberonbooks
& www.facebook.com/oberonbook